5-MINUTE MUSIC ⚡ PRODUCER

365 MUSIC-MAKING ACTIVITIES

For Better Songwriting and Music Production

BY BRIAN FUNK

For Bog

Welcome to the 5 Minute Music Producer!

Congratulations! You have decided to build habits that will take your music production to the next level!

Each day you are given an activity for you to work on for about 5 minutes.

The exercises in the **5 Minute Music Producer** are designed to create that magic spark of inspiration. They offer a variety of workflows to try. They help you set up resources and tools you can draw upon when you want to create. They help build a library of sounds and ideas you can use in future projects.

Occasionally, I refer to web sites. They are all collected here for your convenience: https://brianfunk.com/5mmp-links

What You Need to Get Started

Music Making Software (DAW) - (I prefer Ableton Live and will occasionally refer to it, but the activities can be completed in any DAW).

A Notebook - There are many writing exercises, so have something to write in. I use pen and paper because I believe I remember what I write more than what I type and I like having the physical object to flip through. But if you prefer a digital tool, that's fine too.

A Reference File System - We will be making a few different on-going lists of ideas that we can refer to when we are creating music. Great songwriters and producers have ideas handy so they don't have to wait for inspiration to strike. Because we want these ideas accessible, I recommend a digital solution you can open any time. The Notes app on your phone works well. A Google Drive folder you can create Docs in is also great. I love the web app, Workflowy (https://workflowy.com).

(Recommended) Project File Organization System - For a long time, I got stressed out about saving my projects because I didn't know what to call them. Now I create a folder for the year. In there are folders for each month. I name my projects by date and something descriptive in the month folders. Example: 2021/ November/ 113021 Fast Guitars. (Here's a tutorial on this subject: https://youtu.be/qng9Dgz8f_o)

While doing the daily activities, here are some things to keep in mind:

Suspend Your Judgement - Don't worry about how good what you are doing sounds. This is the best way to get frustrated. When we worry if our idea sounds good we lose our creative momentum. We start comparing our baby idea to the polished, finished products of our favorite artists. Our baby idea won't stand a chance. You can worry about these things after your song is complete. For now, focus on putting in the time and learning. Trust the process!

Quantity over Quality - The more stuff you make, the more you can afford to take chances and try new ideas. The more you try, the more you learn. The more times you do something, the better you get at doing it. Quantity leads to quality.

It's Not About The Gear - There are exercises that have you recording various sounds for inspiration. While you are welcome to use fancy microphones and high tech contraptions, anything you have available is fine. Modern smart phones have more than adequate internal microphones. Even a recording with a cheap microphone is better than no recording at all. Often I find lo-tech solutions impart character and personality in my music. Don't let gear be an excuse not to work!

Play Like a Child - Embrace a curious mindset of "what happens if I try this?" This will take you into new musical territories.

Have Fun! - You got into music because you love it. Remember that!

And if you feel unmotivated, **remember, it's only 5 minutes!** You can do just about anything for 5 minutes.

———

That's about it! The main job you have is to show up. One of the best ways to build a new habit is to attach it to another habit. So maybe you do these activities before or after one of your daily routines.

Thanks for being part of this journey, and remember, have fun!

Day 1: Music in Arm's Reach

Activity:

Find a few objects within arm's reach that you can make sounds with and record them. (You might be tapping, banging, rubbing, shaking, etc.) Don't overthink it and don't worry about recording quality or background noises. Limit yourself to 5 sounds.

Trim the audio files and make a beat with them. However you choose to work is fine. You might drop the samples into a Drum Rack, a sampler, or just arrange them directly on the grid. Make a few 1 bar patterns.

Takeaway:

One of the goals of these exercises is to show that there is music and inspiration everywhere; we just have to keep our eyes/ears open to noticing it. There's music all around you, all the time. And sometimes background noises add character to a recording.

Day 2: Song Scenarios

It's time to build our first Reference File. Reference Files are lists of ideas we can use in our songs.

Activity:

Make a new Reference File and call it "Song Scenarios."

This is a list of things a person might be doing while listening to your song. Be as specific as possible.

Keep this list handy (Google Docs, Notepad, Workflowy) and add to it any time you think of one. Next time you are trying to come up with an idea for a new song, refer to this list for ideas.

Here's mine. Feel free to steal any you like!

Song Scenarios:
- Driving home late at night after getting dumped
- Laying outside by a pool at a barbecue
- Getting the courage up to ask someone on a date
- Sitting by a fireplace with a lover

- The last dance before the club closes

Takeaway:

We can't always wait for inspiration to strike. Make yourself bottles of inspiration for later. A good music producer is prepared when it's time to produce music. Determining what a listener would be doing when your song is playing will help you make decisions about that song. For instance, you probably won't have a heavy metal song playing while sitting by a fireplace with a lover.

For more on this topic, listen to "What is Your Listener Doing and the 13 Music Emotions" on the Music Production Podcast: https://brianfunk.com/blog/2020/2/6/what-is-your-listener-doing-and-13-musical-emotions-music-production-podcast-151

Day 3: Techniques to Try in a Song

Today, we start another Reference File.

Activity:

Set up a new Reference File and call it "Techniques to Try in a Song."

Make a list of things you can do in a song. I like to add to this list after I watch a new tutorial. Include the link to help you remember the idea. Here's a few of mine you can add to your own:

- Call and Response
- Start with the Chorus
- Control FX with Voice: https://brianfunk.com/blog/2014/11/13/control-fx-with-your-voice-and-create-moving-fx-in-ableton-live
- Use Polyrhythms
- Try unequal loop lengths
- Robot Voice (Vocoder Vocals)
- Easy Percussion: https://brianfunk.com/blog/2015/6/8/2-minute-ableton-tip-easy-percussion

Takeaway:

When it's time to make music, refer to this list to get ideas. I find this list especially helpful after I've come up with an initial idea or short loop. Referring to this list prevents me from stressing out thinking "I don't know what to do next!" Pick something from this list and give it a shot!

Day 4: 3 Presets

Activity:

Open your DAW and choose 3 Instrument presets based on their names. Don't listen to them, just pick them because you like the name (only allow yourself about 30 seconds for this part).

Imagine you were hired to make music with these sounds only. You HAVE to use them. Challenge yourself to make something interesting with them. Pretend you are excited to have these three sounds to work with. The music you make might be outside your normal style. That's the point.

Takeaway:

It's easy to spend hours searching for the perfect sounds. This isn't producing music. This is avoiding producing music. Our limitless options are often the reason we get writer's block. We can come across new ideas and surprises by leaving things to chance.

Day 5: Song Titles

It's time to create another Reference File that will help us keep our ideas handy.

Activity:

Make a new Reference File and call it "Song Titles."

Often just having a song title helps us make decisions about how a song will go and what it will be about. Listen for interesting turns of phrase or expressions to use as song titles. "Eight Days a Week" was something Ringo said once that John and Paul thought was funny. So was "A Hard Day's Night." Maybe it's something your uncle likes to say. Mine likes to laugh and say "I can't win!" It could be a one liner from a movie. "I'll Be Back" from The Terminator also happens to be a Beatles song.

Any time you think of, read, or hear one, add it to your song titles list. The more ideas the merrier.

The next time you are looking for song ideas, refer to this list.

Here's a few of mine. Feel free to steal them!
- A good place to be a bad guy
- The Devil's debt
- The Days are longer than the weeks
- Things never go as planned
- I'm the last man alive
- The Imposter

Takeaway:

When an idea strikes you make sure you get it down. Then have them ready when you are ready to make music.

Day 6: Challenge of 4s

Activity:

Create 4 new tracks in your DAW. On each track you can only play up to 4 different notes (you can play those more than once). See what you can come up with in 5 minutes.

Takeaway:

Limitations force us to find creative solutions. Impose rules and restrictions on yourself to unlock your creativity.

Day 7: Chord Progressions

End of the first week!

By now you should have Reference Files for: Song Scenarios, Techniques to Try in a Song, and Song Titles.

Today we will make another Reference File.

Activity:

Make a new Reference File and call it "Chord Progressions."

Google the titles of a few songs you like and the words "chords" at the end." (Ex: "The Beatles Yesterday chords"). Most of the time you will see the chords without having to even click a link.

Write down the chords to the song, but don't write down the name of the song. The idea is to create a running list of nice chord progressions without an association to the song they came from. This will prevent you from simply recreating or copying the song.

Add to this list any time you hear a song with nice chords.

Takeaway:

Tons of songs have the same chords as other songs. Having a collection of chords you like will help you get started. As this list grows, you will forget which chords go to which songs. You'll be left with lots of cool chord progressions for you to use in your own music.

Quick Review

If you've completed each day of the first week of the 5 Minute Music Producer, congratulations! You're in the process of developing a habit. If not, just start again today. There will most likely be days you miss, but it's no reason to give up!

I want to make sure you have the Reference Files in place. Remember, Reference Files are just lists of ideas you can refer to when making music. By now you should have:

Song Scenarios - Situations a listener might be in that your song would fit.
Song Titles - ideas for song titles and lyrical phrases.
Techniques to Try in a Song - musical ideas you can use in your songs.
Chord Progressions - A list of chord progressions from songs you like.

We will be adding to these throughout the 5 Minute Music Producer, but you should add to them any time an idea strikes. I can tell you from experience that unless I write down my ideas, I almost always forget them! Our Reference Files help us remember our ideas and have them handy when it's time to make music.

Day 8: Try Me

Our modern DAWs come with TONS of devices, samples, templates, and presets. Ableton Live and many other DAWs allow you to create Favorites or Tags within their browsers. In Live these are called Collections; by default they are named after their corresponding color. Using this feature can help you from becoming overwhelmed by choice.

Here's how Collections work in Ableton Live: https://help.ableton.com/hc/en-us/articles/360000268570-Using-Collections-

Activity:

Create a new Collection or Favorite and call it "Try Me." Now spend a few minutes adding presets, plug-ins, samples, and anything else you have that you haven't used much but think will be useful for music making one day. Any time I get a new plug-in or sample pack, I add it to my "Try Me" Collection. "Try Me" is perfect for any time I want to experiment with new tools to reinvigorate my workflow.

Takeaway:

We often hit writer's block when we don't know where to start because there are too many options before us. A "Try Me" Collection is perfect when you don't know where to start and you want something fresh.

Don't let your "Try Me" Collection get too big! That will defeat its purpose. Be selective when adding things, and periodically remove things too.

Day 9: Losses and Failures

Activity:

In your notebook, spend a few minutes making a list of losses and failures (big and small) you've experienced.

Next, go through each one and try to find anything positive from this loss and failure. Were there lessons learned? Did they lead you down a new path in life you might not have explored otherwise? Did they cause you to meet new people or see life in a different way?

Often the hard times make us stronger. These are great topics for songs!

Takeaway:

Pondering our own experiences helps us come up with ideas for songs. Those ideas may manifest in lyrics and/or the overall mood and vibe of a song. Additionally, many great songs have some sort of twist in them that help take the listener on a journey. See if you can find any twists in the plot of your life.

Day 10: A Different Style

One of my favorite lines in literature is from *Hamlet*: "There's nothing either good or bad, but thinking makes it so."

It means that whether or not something is a good or bad thing depends on how we look at it. Things are just things, but our own subjective thoughts make it a positive or a negative. Is it bad that today is a rainy day? Maybe, if you wanted to have a picnic outside. But definitely not, if you are trying to grow vegetables in the middle of drought.

This is why some people love one kind of music and other people hate it.

Activity:

Listen to a popular song outside of your normal styles and genres. If it has found its way to you, there's probably something about it that can be appreciated and learned from. Are the musicians extremely talented? Is the production interesting in some way? Is there a message people are connecting with?

See if you can figure out what it is other people see in it. Write these findings down in your notebook. They might be ideas you can bring to your music.

Takeaway:

There's something to learn from all styles of music, even the ones we may despise. Looking for the good in them can open us up to new ideas and possibilities. We might find something exciting that we don't normally see in our own preferences. And this will help us enjoy and appreciate music of all kinds, even if it isn't something we would choose to put on ourselves.

Day 11: 3 Unused Parts

It's likely that you have a folder of unfinished song ideas. If you are like me, once an idea reaches this folder, it almost never comes out. That's a shame because there are probably some decent ideas in there.

Activity:

Choose 3 unfinished song idea projects. I recommend not even listening to them. Drag one element from each song idea into a new project. See if you can make something new with these 3 different parts from 3 different songs.

(Ableton Live allows you to drag tracks from one Live Set directly into another Live Set. Here's how to do it: https://help.ableton.com/hc/en-us/articles/360001830524-Merging-Live-Sets)

Takeaway:

When we are stuck trying to come up with a new idea, we can use some of our old ideas. Using a drum track from an old unfinished idea (especially if we don't listen to the old idea first) can be just the spark we need. Maybe we abandoned that old idea because everything we added after that drum track was garbage. Think of the elements from your abandoned ideas as material for new ideas.

In this video, I use this technique to save valuable set up time: https://brianfunk.com/blog/reusing-tracks

Day 12: Sensory Imagery

Sensory Imagery is descriptive language that uses any of the five senses (sight, hearing, smell, taste, touch).

Our five senses are how we experience the world. Without them, how would we know what is going on around us? How would we even know anything is going on around us at all?

Describing the input your five senses are receiving helps people understand what it was like to experience what you are writing about.
Notice how much more real sensory imagery can make our writing:

No sensory imagery - I'm nervous.

With sensory imagery - A bead of sweat drips down my forehead (touch and sight). My nerves are racing (touch). I hear my heart beating through my chest (hearing). Hands shaking like a leaf (sight).

Activity:

Look at your Reference File "Song Scenarios." Choose one of them and describe it in your notebook, using the five senses. The example I created above was using my song scenario "Getting up the courage to ask someone on a date."

Takeaway:

The key to making people feel your lyrics is sensory imagery. Use it to bring your writing to life!

Day 13: A Song You Love

Let's add to our Reference File "Techniques to Try in a Song."

Activity:

Put on a song you love. As you listen, make a list in your notebook of all of the things you enjoy about it.

Be as specific as possible. "Cool intro" won't help much. "Starts with a distant piano and some street noise" is a specific idea you can use or alter for your own music.

Add these ideas to your Reference File "Techniques to Try in a Song."

Takeaway:

Listening to music is one of the best ways to get inspired to make music. There are great ideas for our songs living in the songs we love. Pay attention to them and try them in your music.

Day 14: Headlines

You've been doing the 5 Minute Producer for 2 weeks! Great job!

Let's add to our Reference File "Song Titles."

Activity:

Spend a few minutes browsing newspaper headlines. You can get a local newspaper or just browse them online. Often they contain catchy phrases and puns. Look for ones that would make interesting song titles and add them to your list. You might alter them in some way, removing or adding words.

Takeaway:

An interesting title can come from all kinds of places. Headlines have been a source of inspiration to artists since the printed word began. It's because a good headline gets your attention and makes you want to read the article. Learn from them and use them in your songs.

Day 15: Beat Body

Activity:

Make a beat using your body! Snap your fingers, clap your hands, slap your thighs, pound your chest, rub your hands together, scratch your head, etc.

Trim the audio files and arrange them into a beat or put them together in a Drum Rack or sampler of choice. Feel free to change their pitches and time-stretch them. Now make a few 1 bar loops with them.

Takeaway:

Today is a reminder that there is music everywhere. These sounds might work really well on their own or when combined with more traditional sounds. The cool part is that these are sounds only you could make with your own unique body!

Day 16: Defining Elements

We often get stuck after making a loop because we don't have a clear vision for our song. A great way to give our songs direction is to have a defining element.

Let's add some defining elements to our "Techniques to Try in a Song" Reference File.

Activity:

Think of some of your favorite songs. It's likely there's something that happens that sticks out. "Yesterday" is the Beatles song with just Paul and the string quartet. "In the Air Tonight" has Phil Collins' iconic drum fill. Pick 3 songs you love and figure out a defining element and write them down in your "Techniques to Try in a Song" Reference File. It's possible the defining element might be an artist's trademark. It's ok to write those down too! Also, you be might be the only person that notices the defining element. Again, write it down!

If you have some extra time today, why not create a song with that particular defining element? Or work that element into an existing idea!

Takeaway:

We aren't trying to copy songs and artists. We are using their ideas as inspiration. Countless songs have done this in the past. We all stand on the shoulders of giants.

Day 17: Forget You Are Recording

Pressing the record button can be scary. We get nervous and stiff, and our performances suffer. I know I will often keep stopping at every small mistake, delete what I recorded, and start it over, a little more frustrated and insecure every time.

So when I am trying to come up with ideas, I hit record and let it run. I play, make mistakes, and keep going. I forget that I am recording and just play around for a while.
Then after a few minutes, and once I think there may be some good moments, I go back and listen for small phrases that I like. Sometimes I find a few consecutive bars I like, other times I stitch together some good notes I find at various points in the recording.

Activity:

Find a small piece of music you have left unfinished and let it loop. Maybe you use the loops you created on Day 15: Beat Body. It doesn't matter; don't overthink it.

Load an instrument or set up a microphone and hit record. Then just play. Have fun. Try things out. After a few minutes, stop and listen back. Try to find a couple of bars you like or stitch together a few notes and phrases into a couple of bars.

Takeaway:

This is one of my favorite ways to come up with new parts for a song. It's important to just let it record so you capture everything. You might find a part and need to edit it, quantize it, tune it, or just re-record it. It takes the pressure out of recording and helps you get back to having fun and playing.

I do this with bands I play in as well. We record everything we do and then we either listen back at the end of practice when everyone is tired or I send my band members a copy of the recording. We listen for parts that work well and develop them further next time.

Day 18: Freewriting

Freewriting is an exercise writers do to get ideas on paper without any judgment. You just write whatever comes to mind for a certain period of time. It's an attempt to capture your thoughts on paper as quickly as possible. The goal is to keep the pen moving the entire time. If your mind wanders, let the pen follow. Don't be afraid to leave thoughts unfinished. Don't read what you wrote until the time is up. Don't edit. Don't worry about phrasing things elegantly. This is a quantity over quality exercise.

Activity:

Set a timer for 3 minutes and free write until it goes off (You could go longer but these activities are meant to be done in about 5 minutes!). You can start by writing about something interesting you did recently or a problem you are trying to solve. But just write the thoughts as they come to your head without filtering them.

If you are thinking you don't know what to write, write those thoughts. "I don't know what to write. I can't think of anything. Nothing interesting has happened in a week." Your mind will wander from that eventually!

Pretend it's a contest to write as many words as possible.
When the timer goes off, spend the next few minutes looking over what you wrote for any good song ideas. Underline interesting phrases. You may decide to focus on writing more about an idea that came up.

See if anything you wrote can be added to one of your Reference Files (probably Song Scenarios or Song Titles).

Takeaway:

A lot of times we feel like we don't have anything to say. But we all live in a never ending flow of thoughts, worries, concerns, emotions, urges, etc. Freewriting is a great way to notice them and harvest them for inspiration.

Day 19: The Number One Song

Activity:

Look up what the number one song in your area is. Listen to it and make a list of things you notice about it while listening. See if there are any ideas you can borrow. Add any ideas to your Reference Files (Song Scenarios, Chord Progressions, Song Titles, Techniques to try in a song).

At the time of writing this, Taylor Swift's "All Too Well" is the number one song in America, according to Billboard. Here's some notes I wrote:

Creaky piano noises.
Breathy, intimate vocal.
Only piano and vocal in first verse.
Bass and vocal harmony enter in chorus
1-5-6-4 Chord progression
Distant spacey synth in the background in second verse
Very specific lyrics to convey a point "I left my scarf there at your sister's house and you still got it in your drawer"

(I didn't realize I was listening to a "From the Vault" version, but I still think there are some valuable ideas here. Plus, I actually enjoyed it more than the album version!)

Takeaway:

Even if you aren't a fan of popular music, there's a lot we can learn from it. Often it's created by a team of extremely talented and experienced people. There's got to be something interesting to learn from. This is an exercise we will revisit once in a while.

Day 20: Misuse Your Instruments

Activity:

Pick a musical instrument and figure out untraditional ways to use it.

For example: tapping on different parts of the body for percussion, manipulating mechanical parts (pressing buttons or flipping switches on a synth), singing into it (I love the sound of vocals sung directly into hot guitar pickups. I've also used my piano as a sort of reverb by holding the sustain pedal and singing at the strings.), etc. If the computer is your only instrument, see what sounds you can make with it (keyboard keys, mouse clicks, plugging and unplugging wires from the ports, etc.).

Once you have a few sounds, experiment with them in your DAW. Try cutting the sounds up and making a beat. Pitch-shift them. Put them in a sampler. Run them through a series of effects.

Have fun and play! You might come up with some unique sounds for your songs!

Takeaway:

This is another "there's music everywhere" type of exercise. It's also a reminder to look at our instruments with a different perspective. Unorthodox approaches lead to new ideas.

Day 21: Write About Your Song

Activity:

Look at your "Song Titles" Reference File and pick one title that strikes you.
Now spend the next few minutes making up the story for this song in your notebook. Think about answering the questions: Who, What, When, and Where. A story without a conflict is not a story. What are the conflicts in your song? What is the climax in your song? Often some kind of twist makes things interesting; can you think of one?

Write as much as you can. Think of this exercise as a focused freewrite: the more the better. You don't have to keep every idea. You might find some phrases that can become lyrics. The stuff you don't use might be useful in other songs.

Takeaway:

The point of this exercise is to flesh out an idea and see it clearly. This can help you make musical decisions as well.

Day 22: Reply Songs

Activity:

Pick a song you like that is about another person. Google the lyrics. Write a reply to this song from the other person's perspective. It might help to follow the format of the original song. For example, if the verse is 8 lines and the chorus is 2 alternating lines that repeat, you can copy that structure. You can make it an obvious reply or be a little more stealthy; it's up to you!

Takeaway:

We can always use songs we love as inspiration. This technique has been the fuel for many great songs. Neil Young's "Southern Man" and "Alabama" helped birth Lynyrd Skynyrd's reply, "Sweet Home Alabama." Rappers often create diss tracks, which inspire their targets to write replies.

Here's a list of reply songs: https://www.everyhit.com/answer/

Day 23: Write Around the Rhymes

Activity:

Go to an online rhyming dictionary. I like https://www.rhymer.com . Enter a key word that relates to your song idea. Jot down any interesting rhymes. Enter a few more related words and repeat the process.

Now that you have a bunch of rhymes, try to construct the lyrics around the rhyme.

Takeaway:

Sometimes we need a little bit of chance to help us come up with ideas. By starting with words that rhyme, we already have the ending of our lines. Now we can fill in the rest of the lyrics around those rhymes.

Day 24: Keep it Simple

I often get stuck in my writing when I am trying to be clever about it. Let's experiment with being extremely simple.

Activity:

Make a chord progression using only two chords. Don't take more than a minute or two picking out the chords. Then immediately start building on top of it. Try starting with a melody. Instead of having the melody last the length of the two chords, make it last for two repetitions of these chords. For example, if your two-chord progression is 2 bars long, make your melody 4 bars long. This will give your chord progression the effect of feeling longer. You can use this same concept on other elements, like the bass for instance.

Takeaway:

Letting go of being fancy and smart about our writing can help us move forward. We worry less about if we are being clever and more about just making something. Once we have some ideas, we can create clever elements. But trying to be clever in the first place might make you throw out decent ideas before they have a chance to develop.

Day 25: Anaphora

Anaphora is the repetition of the first few words of a phrase. Those repeated words are then completed with a different ending. Anaphora makes the listeners/readers predict what you are about to say. It has a subconscious effect of creating harmony with them, because they know what to expect. Listeners/readers that feel harmonious with you are more likely to believe you and be convinced by you. In music, it's another way to make our lyrics more memorable and more catchy.

Some famous examples of anaphora:

Martin Luther King Jr.'s "I Have a Dream" speech. King repeats the phrase "I have a dream" to create hope and optimism, while painting a picture of what a more harmonious world will look like.

John Lennon's "God." Lennon repeats "I don't believe in…" numerous times before ending with "I just believe in me."

Pete Seeger's "Turn, Turn, Turn"
"A time to be born, a time to die

A time to plant, a time to reap
A time to kill, a time to heal
A time to laugh, a time to weep"

Activity:

Try to create some lyrics using anaphora. Look at your Song Titles Reference File or at some of the writing in your notebook for phrases to repeat. If you are struggling to come up with any, here's a few to pick from:

I never knew...
You always said...
When I was young...

Takeaway:

Songs are catchy because of the way they repeat. We can use this in our lyrics, and anaphora is an excellent technique.

Day 26: Your Influence's Influences

Activity:

Google one of your favorite artists and see if you can find out who their influences are. You might find this information in an interview or an album/song review. Listen to a song by your influence's influence and look at some pictures of them. In your notebook, write down anything you can learn from this artist. Why do you think they had an impact on your influence? What parts do you like and what parts do you dislike? Put yourself in the shoes of your influence and see if you can find any inspiration in the people that inspired them.

If you like the chord progression, Google it or figure it out on your instrument, then add it to your Reference File "Chord Progressions."

If there were any interesting musical moments add them to your Reference File "Techniques to Try in a Song."

Takeaway:

Even the most original artists have influences. We can learn a lot from our influence's influences, and it can help us understand our own personal musical heritage.

Day 27: Record Conversation

Activity:

Record a minute or two of people talking. It could be a conversation you are having or you can lurk in the background of a conversation other people are having and record them (don't get in yourself in trouble). Look for any interesting phrases or expressions. Keep it short. Chop up the words and make a rhythmic repeating beat out of the words. It might help to do this over a drum beat or instrumental (this is a great way to add life to an unfinished idea). You can repitch or time-stretch the voices. You might Auto-Tune them or layer them on top of each other. See if you make something interesting with the conversation.

Takeaway:

Often conversations have a natural flow and rhythm to them. People say things in interesting ways and use turns of phrase that might work well in a song. You can take parts of these conversations out of context and use them in your music. I like to collect little phrases and bits of talk so I can add them into my music when I want a little more humanity or some excitement.

Day 28: Write About a Song You Love

About a week ago we did an exercise where we wrote the story of a song idea. Today we will do it with a song we love.

Activity:

Pick a song you love. Look up the lyrics. In your notebook, write about the story of the song. Consider who, what, when, and where. What is the high point of the song? Are there any twists and unexpected turns? How does the music interact with the lyrics?

Write as much as you can. Don't worry about making incorrect assumptions about the song. This isn't about getting it right, it's about your interpretation of it. Your misinterpretation could always be used in one of your songs.

If you come across any ideas for titles, techniques to try, chord progressions, or song scenarios, add them to your Reference Files!

Takeaway:

Breaking down our favorite songs can help us understand how to construct our own. Pay attention to what your favorite artists are doing and adapt those ideas to your own music!

Day 29: Opposite Songs

Activity:

Take a look at a playlist of songs. You might search your Spotify or Apple Music Libraries, or just Google for some kind of list. I Googled "100 Greatest Rock Songs" and came across a list from Rolling Stone magazine. Look for any titles that you can create an opposite of. Add these to your Reference File "Song Titles."

Here's a few of my opposites (as always, feel free to use them):

"I Will Survive" -> "I Won't Survive"
"Just Like Heaven" -> "Just Like Hell"
"Time to Pretend" -> "Time to Get Real"
"All Apologies" -> "No Apologies"
"It's Your Thing" -> "It's Not Your Thing"

Takeaway:

A lot of times a good idea is still a good idea if you flip it around. Experimenting with opposites is a great way to find something new. I read that Joy Division came up with "Love Will Tear Us

Apart" after "Love Will Keep Us Together." So cool!

Day 30: Music with Plants

Activity:

Make music with plants! Record as many sounds as you can with plants. Rustle the leaves. Tap on tree trunks. Crumple dried leaves. Make a whistle with a blade of grass: https://youtu.be/qc9Zc2g9D94 Be creative, but try not to hurt the plant!

Trim the audio files and arrange them into a beat or put them together in a Drum Rack. Feel free to change their pitches and time-stretch them. Now make a few 1 bar loops with them.

Takeaway:

Let Mother Nature help you make music. This type of exercise is great for making your music sound more organic!

Day 31: Showing Not Telling

Classic advice given to writers all the time is "show don't tell." Telling doesn't impact us much, but showing us brings us in the moment by supplying us with the details that make up an experience.

Activity:

Pick a topic you want to write about. Perhaps you look at your "Song Scenarios" Reference File. Now write about the situation without telling what the situation is. Focus on the details. It's almost like putting together clues for the reader to piece together. Let the reader come to the conclusion on their own.

Bruce Springsteen does this on "Used Cars" to show the nervousness and tension of a family test driving a new used car they may not be able to afford.

"My little sister's in the front seat with an ice cream cone
My ma's in the backseat sittin' all alone
As my pa steers her slow out of the lot for a test drive down Michigan Avenue

Now my ma she fingers her wedding band
And watches the salesman stare at my old man's hands
He's tellin' us all 'bout the break he'd give us if he could but he just can't"

The details of the wedding band and the salesman staring at his father's hands capture the nervousness without telling us they are nervous. He paints a picture rather than telling us about the picture.

Takeaway:

When we are forced to sort out the details ourselves, we feel it more. If you want to move people with your lyrics, show them what it was like. The small details are what make up all of our experiences.

Day 32: Stop Listening

Activity:

Try to make some music without listening to it as you make it. Pick a drum kit and two melodic instruments and load them into tracks. Write 2 bar loops for each track by entering in notes in the piano roll. But don't listen to it! Mute your speakers or just don't allow the notes to play. Spend a few minutes making as many short loops as you want, then stop and listen back.

Takeaway:

Sometimes it's nice to put ourselves out of our normal comfort zones and see what we can make. It's likely that writing music without hearing it will lead to unexpected results. There might be a fun surprise that gets you excited about the idea. You are free to edit things once you start listening.

Day 33: It's Not This, It's That

Antithesis is a statement that contains a contrast of two ideas. Often delivered in the format of "It is not this, it is that."

Activity:

Refer to your Reference Files "Song Scenarios" and "Song Titles" and pick one of the topics. Make a list of the good things and the bad things about the topic. Then start using these as lyrics. Try setting up lyrics in the form of 3 lines of "It's not…(negative things)" and a 4th line of "It's… (positive thing). You could of course organize the lines in any manner you wish.

Takeaway:

Parents do this so effectively with "I'm not angry; I'm disappointed." It sets up the listener in one direction and then takes them another way. Antithesis is a great way to make a statement by creating contrast and opposites. Contrast and opposites are great ways to create tension and release, build up and pay off, which are all part of creating impactful music.

Day 34: The Outsider

Activity:

In your notebook, write about times you've felt like an outsider. Start with just a list. Then choose something from that list and go into detail about it. Answer the who, what, when, where, and whys. Then move on to sensory imagery (using the five senses in your descriptive writing). What did you see, hear, smell, taste, and feel? How did people treat you? Think of this writing as fodder for your songs.

Takeaway:

Although when we feel like an outsider we feel completely alone, it is actually a pretty universal feeling. We all feel like outsiders at some point in time, even if just for a few moments. And when we feel this way, a song that deals with the topic can be just the right medicine! Turn your difficult experiences into medicine for others.

Day 35: Don't Worry About the Sounds

Activity:

Load a few basic instruments into some tracks. A simple drum kit, a piano, a bass, and some kind of melody instrument. Don't worry so much about the sounds, just make sure they are extremely simple and possibly a bit boring.

Save this as a template in your DAW. (Here's how to do it in Ableton Live: https://help.ableton.com/hc/en-us/articles/209067189-Creating-new-or-blank-Template-Sets)

Now try to come up with a short piece of music using only these sounds for now.

Takeaway:

Any DAW comes with a nearly endless selection of sounds to work with. Sometimes we get stuck just looking for the right sound. There's really no right sound though. It all depends on the song. By completely bypassing the searching stage, we focus on the music itself instead of relying on sounds. Once we have a few ideas, we can replace our sounds with more appropriate ones. But for now, cut straight to the music making.

Day 36: A Song Like That

Activity:

Listen to a song you loved as a teenager. In your notebook, take notes on what it is you loved about it when you were young. What do you hear that you might not like if you first heard the song today? What is the message of the song? Does it still resonate? Does the song resonate in a new way? Are there interesting musical things happening that you can try in your songs?

Look for anything that you can add to your Reference Files. Song Titles, Techniques to Try in a Song, and Chord Progressions can all be sourced using songs that you loved.

Takeaway:

Studying songs we love can give us ideas for our own songs. By looking back on songs that had an impact on us, we can tap into emotions and situations we haven't thought about in a while and use them in our songs!

Day 37: The Hyperbole

Hyperbole is the technique of using an extreme exaggeration to get a point across.

Activity:

Take a look at your Reference Files "Song Titles" and "Song Scenarios." Pick one that you can exaggerate. Often catchy lyrics and musical ideas can come out of exaggerations. How might you exaggerate the lyrics? Can you think of ways the music might reflect this? Try to construct a song with these ideas in play.

Some examples of songs with Hyperbole:

"Gonna Be (500 Miles)" by The Proclaimers ("I would walk 500 hundred miles…)
"So Happy I Could Die" by Lady Gaga

Takeaway:

By creating exaggerations, we can really emphasize our points. Think about exaggerations in the music too. If there's a quiet section, make it as quiet as possible, so the loud section feels louder. If the lyric says "Stop!" trying stopping the music.

If the lyrics use the word "down" try moving the melody down too. Think of ways to help exaggerate the messages to make them more memorable.

Day 38: Try it a Different Way

Activity:

How do you normally begin a song? Drums? Chords? Melody? Lyrics?

Today, do it another way. What would be the most opposite approach to yours? Try it! What is the last thing you normally work on? Do that first! This will take you out of your comfort zone and force you to see songwriting and music production in a different light.

Takeaway:

It's great to have workflows and patterns to create. So much of this course is about discovering them for ourselves so we can employ them. But temporarily putting them aside can open up new possibilities. You might find that another approach forces you to write in a new way. With a little practice, this might also become a workflow you rely on.

Day 39: Write a Theme Song

Activity:

Pick a character from a movie you love. In your notebook, brainstorm the character's situation and conflicts. You might even write down some memorable quotes from the character. We are trying to find interesting angles for our own songs. Often our favorite characters are going through specific problems that ring true in a universal way. See if you can create a theme song that encapsulates what the character is going through.

Add any clever lines or thoughtful perspectives to your "Song Titles" and "Song Scenario" Reference Files.

Takeaway:

We don't always have to live through situations ourselves to use them as inspiration for songs. If a story you encounter strikes you, capture it in song.

Day 40: Mix It Up

Activity:

Move yourself from your normal music-making area. Make an event out of it. If the weather permits, try sitting outside. Go to a park. If you are working in the computer, get some headphones, go to a coffee shop and treat yourself to a fancy beverage. Try a different place in your home or visit a friend or family member's place where you can do a little work.

Takeaway:

A different environment pulls our mind from its normal pattern of thinking. You will literally see things in a different way and notice new things to write music about. Additionally, it puts you in the frame of thinking "I am here to work." When you are done, consider how the environment may have affected what you made.

Day 41: Action and Description

Weave action into your descriptions. Our writing will be more exciting if we combine description with action. A great way to do this is by starting sentences with words like "as, before, during, and while" or with present-tense verbs ("-ing" verbs).

Here are a few examples:

As I reach for the doorknob, I feel our relationship disintegrating.
During the commotion, she reached for his hand.
Driving through the city, nostalgia washed over me.

Activity:

Write about something you did recently and try to create sentences with both action and description. Don't worry about the subject matter so much as the exercise of weaving action into your descriptions.

Takeaway:

Exciting writing has action. Practice this in your writing. And remember, you may be writing interesting sentences and lines that can be used as lyrics of a song!

Day 42: Write Someone Else's Song

Activity:

Think of the last movie/tv show/play you watched or book you read. Write down a problem the main character was having. Be specific. Include specific details from the situation. Now see if you can come up with a song for that character. Use the character's situation to determine if your song is happy or sad, fast or slow, a certain genre or style, etc.

If you are able to come up with a solid song idea, great. If not, look for ideas you can add to any of your Reference Files, especially the Song Scenario one.

Takeaway:

You don't always have to be the subject of your songs. It can be liberating to take on the perspective of someone else. I've found this approach actually helps me tap into more universal ideas and themes. Even though I may not have been in the exact situation myself, it's likely I've felt similar emotions.

Below are lyrics to a song I wrote with my band after watching a reality television show called *90 Day Fiancé*. One of the people on the show was sending money to a woman he never met on the other side of the world. To everyone in his life, he was being scammed, but he was convinced it was love. The lyrics here are from the perspective of someone who feels that on the infinite scale of the universe, to even be on the same planet at the same time with a love interest must mean it's destiny. It's a delusional song but I think we can all relate to the feeling that someone who doesn't know we exist is destined to be ours. (PS I know Mercury doesn't have any moons. But the line sings well and sort of adds to the faulty logic of the narrator!).

Universe

I had an epiphany
In terms of the Galaxy:
Since you're on Earth with me,
It's like you're right next to me.

Compared to Jupiter

Or the moons of Mercury
Talk about proximity
On the Pale Blue Dot with me

Run around the universe with you baby
Run around the universe with you girl
Run around the universe with you baby
Staring at the stars shining in your eyes

What a coincidence
Everything's making sense
Our synchronicity
It's no mystery

I don't care what they say to me
I know I'm your Destiny
They put you on the Earth for me
Together for infinity and beyond

Run around the universe with you baby
Run around the universe with you girl
Run around the universe with you baby

Staring at the stars shining in your eyes

Day 43: Use Your Name

Open the Musical Note Coder (Located at the end of this book).

Each letter of the alphabet has a corresponding musical note.

Activity:

Use your first name to come up with a collection of musical notes. You can use your last name if your first is too short or too long. These are the notes you are allowed to make music with today. What can you come up with?

Takeaway:

You can use the Musical Note Coder to give yourself a starting place for your music. It can be especially fun to code secret messages into your music!

Day 44: Your Hometown

Activity:

Spend a few minutes free writing about your hometown. Think about the specific places, the specific people, and the specific events. As with any free write, write down whatever comes to mind.

Once you are done, review your writing for any interesting lines or topics that you can add to your Reference Files.

Takeaway:

Many great songs were written about people's hometowns. We can all relate to reminiscing about our old stomping grounds. It's a great subject matter for songs. Share yours with the world!

Day 45: Your Zip Code

Open the Numeric Note Coder (Located at the end of this book).

Let's run with the "Hometown" idea from yesterday and compose a melody using our zip code/postal code.

Activity:

Write down your hometown's zip code. Let's say mine was 31702. Choose a scale. Each digit of the number will represent a note in a melody. In C Major that would become E C B C D. Use those notes, in that order, to write a melody.

Takeaway:

We have now coded our hometown's zip code into a melody. This method can help you decide on notes and incorporate secret codes in your melodies.

Day 46: Your First Phone Number

Let's keep the "Hometown" idea going and compose a melody with our first phone number.

Open the Numeric Note Coder (Located at the end of this book).

Activity:

Write down your first phone number, preferably the one you had when you lived in your hometown. Stay within the same key as yesterday and use the Numeric Note Coder to write a melody with your home phone number. If my phone number was 587-6435, my notes in C Major would be G C B A F E G. Use the notes you come up with to write an additional melody for yesterday's idea.

Takeaway:

By using different elements from our past, we are coming up with a few coded melodies that would work perfectly for a song about our hometown.

Day 47: Putting it all Together

Activity:

Let's take the ideas we came up with from Days 43-46 and combine them to make a full song. You've come up with melodies using your name, zip code, and phone number. Think of these as three different parts of your song (perhaps verse, chorus, bridge). You've also written about your hometown. Try to structure something using all of these parts. (And don't forget, don't worry about how good it is. Think of it more as reaching the goal of completing a song using constraints and limitations).

Takeaway:

A lot of times, we can combine ideas from different sessions to create a single composition. Of course, if you wound up with 4 different song ideas, great! Try to complete any of those. Many artists have combined small ideas to come up with something big (just listen to the second half of *Abbey Road* by the Beatles!)

Day 48: Madlibs

Remember Madlibs? They were stories with keywords removed and they would ask you for nouns, verbs, adverbs, etc. that you would fill in the blanks with. The results were often silly and almost nonsensical. (Here's a review if you aren't familiar with Madlibs: https://www.madlibs.com)

Also here are the basic parts of speech in case you need a refresher: https://mrbfunk.wordpress.com/parts-of-speech/

Activity:

Pick a song you like the lyrics to. Write them out but remove the nouns and verbs. Choose a Song Title from your Reference List. Replace those nouns and verbs with words that go with your song title.

You can alter lines as much as you want. And the more you alter the less it will resemble the original lyrics. See if you can get it to a point where the original is no longer recognizable.

Takeaway:

This is another example of using existing material to create our own new material. This technique can make it much easier to get started and will also provide some structure and organization for your own ideas.

Day 49: Using Your Voice as an Instrument

Activity:

Set up an audio track and a microphone. If you don't have a microphone, you can use your computer's built-in microphone (The quality isn't important today. Just make sure you are using headphones so you don't get feedback).

Load up an auto-tune device (here's a fun free one: https://www.auburnsounds.com/products/Graillon.html)

After the auto-tune, put some kind of amp simulation or distortion effect. The goal is to make your voice sound less like a voice and more like an instrument.

Now have fun trying to come up with catchy melodies! You might try this over some chords you have written previously (like an old unfinished idea).

Takeaway:

Catchy tunes are easy to sing and hum along with. If you write them with your voice, it's likely they are easy to sing along with. I've found this technique really useful because I don't have to worry about singing well and I don't have to worry about the words I sing. It's just the adventure of finding nice melodies.

Imagine Dragons mention using this technique in this interview (includes before and after audio examples): https://www.ableton.com/en/blog/imagine-dragons-from-home-studio-to-shangri-la/

Day 50: A Song of Celebration!

Wow! You've made it to Day 50 of the 5-Minute Music Producer. That's an incredible accomplishment. Sticking with something this long is not easy and I hope you recognize some growth in your music and work habits.

Today let's make a song of celebration!

Activity:

Add "Celebration of a Victory" to your Song Scenarios Reference Files.

Spend the next few minutes freewriting about victories and winning. You can think about times you have triumphed (like making it to Day 50!) and times you've witnessed others succeed (sports teams, friends, family, etc.). Try to come up with some specific details about celebrations. They don't need to be related. And as always just write whatever comes to mind; don't judge yet!

A few ideas to get you started:

Champagne soaked uniform
Golden trophy shining in the stadium lights.

The crack of a solid high five.
Tears of joy mixing with the sweat on your cheeks.

[Notice how these details use Sensory Imagery (the use of any of the five senses in a description). Sensory Imagery can help bring the details to life.]

Takeaway:

There are certain occasions that repeatedly happen in people's lives. Fortunately, victories are one of them. Maybe you can create a song people will put on at their next glorious achievement!

Day 51: A Roll of the Dice

Activity:

Go to Google's "Roll Dice" page: https://g.co/kgs/M1Hfzc

Choose the 8-sided Die. (You can use a real die if you have one)

Roll 4 times.

Use these numbers to create a chord progression in a key of your choice. For example, if I rolled 3, 5, 2, and 8, in the key of C major, this would translate to E minor, G major, D minor, and C major.

Takeaway:

It's always a great exercise to try to make interesting music out of whatever is presented before you. This activity is a lot like working with a collaborator who has a song idea. Your job is to help build something with it.

Day 52: The Locrian Challenge

I've heard it said that the Locrian Mode is the least useful of the Modes of Major. Let's see if we can make use of it!

If you are unfamiliar with Locrian, use the notes of C Locrian: C D♭ E♭ F G♭ A♭ B♭.

Activity:

Try to write a bit of music using the Locrian Mode. Embrace the tension and dissonance of this mode. It can help to imagine you are making some music for a film.

Takeaway:

I think people dislike using the Locrian Mode because it's so dissonant. I find it difficult to write in, but I have found it allows me to create moods and emotions that I don't normally try to create. Experimenting with it has helped me realize that it can be useful for certain moods. You might just tap into something interesting!

Day 53: Oblique Strategies

Brian Eno created a set of cards for creative inspiration called "Oblique Strategies." Each card has an abstract statement that is meant to be used to help inspire creativity.

Activity:

Visit the Oblique Strategies online here: http://stoney.sb.org/eno/oblique.html

Each time you load the page you will get a new "card."

Use the "card" you get to come up with some music. It will be up to you to interpret the meaning of the card and how to apply it. This might be a bit challenging, but be as creative as possible!

Takeaway:

When I loaded the page, I got "Change Instrument Roles." I interpret this as "use your instrument in an unusual way." So now I'm thinking about using guitar as percussion (disco music did this well with a wah wah pedal and muted string strums to create those "wack-a wack-a" rhythms). Phil Collins has a sort of lead drum part in "In the Air Tonight." What will you come up with?!

Day 54: A Random Word

Activity:

Go to https://randomwordgenerator.com/noun.php and get a random noun to focus on. Spend the next few minutes free writing about this noun. Whatever comes to mind is perfect. After a few minutes, look to see if there are any interesting phrases or story ideas you can use for a song. Collect these in your Song Titles and Song Scenarios Reference Files.

I got the word "crumb." In my free write I came up with the phrase "sweep up the broken pieces and hide them from view" which became the start of a new song.

Takeaway:

The random noun you get is really inconsequential. It's just a focused starting place. It can be difficult to start when there is no direction, but having something to begin with is often enough for the mind to start coming up with ideas.

Day 55: Use Movie Titles

Activity:

Browse through some movie titles. You might go to Netflix or simply Google a list of classic movies. Choose one and start brainstorming about it in your notebook. Try applying the title to a situation in your life. You might even alter the movie title a bit. Can you make an opposite title? What if you switched out a word or added/removed one? What kind of situation would this title apply to?

Capture any good ideas in your Reference files for Song Titles and Song Scenarios.

Takeaway:

Movie titles need to be interesting and captivating so people will want to watch them. You can use them to generate ideas for your songs. I like this approach for movies I've never seen. I try to imagine what the story behind the title might be and if it's interesting to me, try to write a song around it.

Day 56: Record First

Check out this video I did for Ableton's "One Thing" series: https://brianfunk.com/blog/ableton-one-thing

Activity:

Find a plug-in, instrument, or device of some kind that is unfamiliar to you. Start recording and play around with it for a few minutes. Record before you really understand how to use the device. This will ensure that you capture any happy accidents you might make as a beginner, that you won't make once you actually know what you are doing.

Takeaway:

This process is really handy for opening up new ways of working. One of the things I love about new gear is that it helps me work in new ways. But often, I fall into patterns with that piece of gear. Using the "Record First" workflow might unlock some new ideas you wouldn't normally have.

Day 57: Build the Band

One of the nice things about playing in a traditional band is that the instrumentation and the roles are predetermined. You don't need to figure out what instruments to use and how to use them. In modern production, these options are endless and often paralyzing.

Activity:

Spend some time building your band. Choose instruments that will fill up your rhythm section. Determine what sounds will function as your leads. Save these tracks as a template you can use when inspiration strikes.

Takeaway:

Sometimes the difference between capturing ideas and missing them is the set up. Inspiration is fleeting and if it takes a few minutes to get ready to capture them, they may already have gotten away. Having a few "Bands" to turn to at a moment's notice can make all the difference.

Day 58: A Sound You'd Never Use

Activity:

Open an instrument, synth, or drum machine and try to find a sound you would never use. Spend the next few minutes trying to make music with it. You are free to use other sounds with it.

Takeaway:

Think of this one as a challenge. Can you make music with a sound you don't like? At worst, this will strengthen your ability to make lemonade from lemons. At the very least, you will make a piece of music you wouldn't have made otherwise. It's easy to get stuck on sounds we like and fall into predictable patterns. Mixing it up with a sound you'd never use might open up new possibilities.

Day 59: Mama Used to Say

Activity:

Try to think of something an elder would say to you when you were young. Write it down in your notebook and spend a few minutes brainstorming about it. What was the context? Do you agree or disagree with it? How can you apply it to your life now? Were there times you wished you followed/didn't follow this advice? Be specific!

Review what you have written for any ideas for songs. Are there interesting lines or titles? Are there any situations you've uncovered that you can write about?

Add these to your Reference Files, particularly Song Titles and Song Scenarios.

Takeaway:

We are looking for wisdom today. Often this type of wisdom makes for interesting song ideas, especially choruses. Some examples: "Mama said there'd be days like this," "Mama said you can't hurry love," "Nobody said it was easy, No one ever said it would be so hard." What's your wisdom song?

Day 60: The Number One Song

Let's see what we can learn from the most popular song right now.

Activity:

Look up what the number one song in your area is. Listen to it and make a list of things you notice about it while listening. See if there are any ideas you can borrow. Add any ideas to your Reference Files (Song Scenarios, Chord Progressions, Song Titles, Techniques to try in a song).

Takeaway:

For a song to reach number one, there has to be something about it that is special. It could be a great melody, an interesting arrangement, or some kind of gimmick. As music producers and songwriters, we should take note of these ideas and learn from them!

Day 61: Object Writing

Object writing is when we freewrite around a specific object. Focus on the five senses. Delve into memories and associations. Personify the object. Give it desires and aspirations. Don't judge what you are writing. Feel free to wander away from the original object. If the pen stops moving, return to the original object and choose one of the five senses to focus on.

Activity:

Spend five minutes doing some object writing. Your object today is: a mirror.

Once you have finished, look for any material that can be used for song ideas. Add these to your Song Titles and Song Scenarios Reference Files. Feel free to explore any interesting lines as song ideas or lyrics. Be on the lookout for lines that you might take out of the context of the original object. Applying the characteristics of one thing to a completely unrelated thing can be the basis for interesting metaphors in your writing.

Takeaway:

Object writing is a great technique for generating ideas. It's meant to be low pressure and free flowing. Don't edit or reread what you've done until the time is up. Let your writing flow without judgment.

Day 62: Cars!

Activity:

Make a beat using a car!

Record a bunch of sounds with a car. Door slamming, trunk closing, horn honking, tapping on the steering wheel and the dashboard, the turning signal… whatever makes a sound.

Trim the audio files and arrange them into a beat or put them together in a Drum Rack. Feel free to change their pitches and time-stretch them. Now make a few 1-bar loops with them.

Takeaway:

There's music everywhere. It's likely you get into a car every day. Notice the sounds around you and use them to make music!

Day 63: Request Inspiration

In his book *War of Art*, Steven Pressfield makes it a point that professional writers cannot wait for inspiration to strike. They must get to work each day with or without its presence.

Part of the point of this book is to do just that. Spend the time each day. You've probably noticed that there were days when you didn't feel like doing it, but after a few minutes you found yourself inspired. Sudden bursts of inspiration are rare, but there are things we can do to inspire it to show up.

Activity:

Listen to one of your favorite songs of the past year. Answer the following questions about it in your notebook, and add some of the answers to your appropriate Reference Files.

What is the general emotion of the song?
In what type of scenario would a person listen to this song?
What are the defining characteristics of the song?
Does the song do anything unexpected?
What is the rhythm and beat like?

What kind of structure does the song have?
What are the chords?
Are there any small ideas touched upon that you could use as a main idea for your song?

This exercise will likely take you the full five minutes. But if you are struck with inspiration, don't let it go to waste! Start making something!

Takeaway:

The best gift another piece of art can give us is the desire to make something ourselves. Pay attention to the details of the music you love and incorporate it into your own music.

Day 64: The Word Ladder

This is an exercise from Jeff Tweedy's book *How to Write One Song*. Sometimes it will seem random and nonsensical. But it works remarkably well for giving unusual actions to objects. It can also give you some interesting ideas to play with.

Activity:

Get two different pieces of writing (these can be anything: a newspaper article, a poem, a novel, a bill statement, etc) In your notebook make two columns. In the left column, write down all the nouns from one piece of writing. In the right column, write down all the verbs from the other piece of writing. Then draw a line from each noun to one of the verbs. From there write ten lines, using the noun-verb combination.

Review what you've written and see if any of the lines inspire ideas. From there, see what you can come up with!

Takeaway:

It helps if you see this as a challenge to make some sort of sense out of random word combinations. I like this writing game because it makes me feel a little less responsible for the content, and therefore less judgmental about what I am writing.

Day 65: Look for Something New

Activity:

Have a look inside your DAW's browser. Look at your plug-ins and presets for any instruments or effects that you haven't spent much time exploring. Way back on Day 8 of this book, we talked about creating a "Try Me" Collection or folder. Add anything you find to this collection. After about a minute of looking, choose one and start trying to work with it. You can open an older, unfinished project and apply it there, or start a new one and see what happens.

Takeaway:

In the digital world, it's very easy to lose sight of our tools. They don't take up any physical space; they just hide in folders. Every once in a while it's a good idea to look for those forgotten tools and see if you can make anything new with them. Often they cause your mind to think in new ways. It may also save you from the temptation of buying something new!

Day 66: Try the Other Side

Activity:

Think of a person you have a difficult relationship with. Now think of a situation or problem you have had with this person. In your notebook, write their side of the story, or at least what you think their side might be. Feel free to exaggerate, imagine, and interpret however you like. It's probably unlikely that they come from a place of malevolence. How might they be justified, even if you disagree with the logic? You might also decide to create a sarcastic interpretation.

Collect any ideas for Song Scenarios and Titles in your Reference Files.

Takeaway:

This might be a difficult exercise. The point is to get you from feeling like you always have to write from your own experience. Writing from the perspective of someone else can unlock many new ideas. It might even get you to understand where the other person is coming from.

Day 67: 8-Bit Style

Early video game composers were stuck with some severe limitations, yet they managed to create some memorable songs that have become embedded in our culture.

Activity:

Limit yourself to only 3 tracks of monophonic melodic sounds. You can have a 4th track for drums and percussion but only allow one percussion sound to play at a time. This is similar to what programmers for the original Nintendo Entertainment System worked with.

Tip: An extremely fast arpeggiator on one of your melodic tracks is great for implying chords!

Takeaway:

Limitations like this can be great for focusing your work. You won't be able to make anything but the main components of your track. This actually worked quite well for many video game composers. If you start making something you really like, you could, of course, add new layers.

But see if you can come up with something interesting first!

Day 68: The Day We Met...

Activity:

Today's work is to use the prompt: "The Day We Met." Write down ideas in your notebook related to this topic.

Before you begin, decide who or what will be the subject of your writing. Maybe it's a lover, an old friend, an enemy... or perhaps it's something nonhuman like music, a pet, or a fast car. If you decide on a nonhuman object, consider giving the object human qualities (wants, desires, movements, attitudes, etc.).

Think about the time and place, who else was there, what activities may have been going on, the weather, what kind of state you were in as a person, etc. Think about your first impressions, as well as what their first impressions might have been. What has changed since you met? What if you never met?

Takeaway:

Many of our lives are permanently changed by chance meetings with others. Dive into those meetings and think about what might be different now. I think the description of the meeting makes for great verse material, while the changes can work nicely as chorus material.

Day 69: Planning "The Day We Met..."

Activity:

Look over what you wrote for yesterday's prompt "The Day We Met."

Jot down some musical ideas that would be appropriate for a song on this topic. What would the emotion be? How fast would the tempo be? Major or Minor key? Something different? Is there a turning point? Is there some type of surprise you could introduce? What instruments would make sense to use?

Takeaway:

Reviewing and coming back to our work a day later often gives us new perspective. Now that we have some ideas written from yesterday, we can plan out the musical ideas that would fit. Tomorrow we can try to apply those ideas!

Day 70: Make the Music

Activity:

Now that we have a solid plan for a song about "The Day We Met," let's start making the music.

Spend some time building up musical ideas. Since this is the 5 Minute Music Producer, work as fast as you can. Say yes to the first ideas that feel even a little good then move on. See if you can put together two sections as quickly as possible, without worrying too much about their quality.

Takeaway:

Sometimes song ideas take a little time to grow. The last few days we have tried an approach that encourages you to get a sense of the "big idea" before moving forward. It often takes a little time for the idea of the song to come together. That's ok! Let things go at their natural pace. You could always work on something else while you wait!

Day 71: Find Some Titles

Activity:

Choose a book you love that you have on hand. It doesn't matter what you choose. Skim through the papers and look for sentences and phrases that might make good titles. Jot these down in your Reference File: "Song Titles."

Takeaway:

Some of my favorite song titles have come from leafing through pages of books I love. Sometimes I alter them a little. I especially like to try the inverse of what is said. Often you get funny turns of phrase that way. A good title should capture the attention of a potential listener, so finding phrases that catch your attention is a great place to start.

Day 72: Just One Instrument

Activity:

Select a sound from your DAW's browser. Use this one sound to make some music. Duplicate it as much as you want, but each track should have the same sound.

Takeaway:

This is a great exercise for composition. It teaches us to use different note ranges in each part of our track. Make a bass sound, create chords, add a lead at a higher pitch. Often our mixes can sound muddy just because we have multiple instruments playing in the same range of notes. When we have the same exact sound for multiple parts, we realize we must play parts using different ranges of notes.

Day 73: Try New Sounds

Activity:

Open yesterday's project where you used the same instrument sound on each track.

Now try replacing some of the tracks with a new sound. See if you can find sounds that fit the notes being played on each track.

Takeaway:

Sometimes we rely on the sound of our instruments to differentiate them from the other tracks in our songs. By first making sure the instruments are playing in different note ranges, when we choose new sounds, often the tracks complement each other better.

Day 74: Paper Sounds

Activity:

Get yourself a piece of paper and make some sounds with it. Slap it, crumple it, tear it, fold it, bang it, write on it… whatever you can think that will make sound. I recommend a sensitive microphone for this so you can capture the smallest of sounds.

Now experiment with those sounds. Chop them, stretch them, change their pitch, reverse them.

Make something rhythmic with them that you can start building a song around.

Takeaway:

Sometimes when we focus on one particular item to make sounds with, we stretch our creative muscles to find new ways to create sounds. See if you can "unlock" the music in ordinary items.

Day 75: Autocomplete Song

Check out this song created with iPhone's autocomplete feature: https://youtu.be/M8MJFrdfGe0

Activity:

Now it's your turn! Use our phone's autocomplete feature to write lyrics. Just tap away for a while until you have a bunch of words. You might actually get some great lines. You might be able to edit them to come up with lyrics. You might even be able to add them to some of your Reference Files, particularly "Song Titles."

Takeaway:

There are music making tools everywhere! Keep your eyes and mind open. Techniques like this could be the perfect way to get a song idea started.

Day 76: Make the Music

Activity:

Now that we have some lyrical ideas after yesterday's auto-complete exercise, let's try to put some music to them. Look for any lines that have an emotion to them and use that as a guide for your music.

Takeaway:

I find it much easier to write music when I have an emotion in mind. Using the auto-complete lyrics method can help come up with some interesting emotions, which usually require a little interpretation and imagination. I find that in hunting for meaning and emotion, my imagination is activated. That is the exact state I want to be in while creating!

Day 77: Uncommon Time Signatures

A large amount of music is created in 4/4 time. Other very common times are 3/4 and 6/8.

Activity:

Challenge yourself to make some music in an uncommon time signature. Try something like 5/4 or 7/4. It helps to divide them in your mind. For example, you can think of 7/4 as a measure of 4 followed by a measure of 3.

Takeaway:

This is another attempt to take us out of our comfort zones. We might end up creating music we wouldn't normally make, which can help us break our predictable patterns.

Day 78: Try an Ostinato

Ostinato is a musical phrase that repeats. Usually the chords or bassline will change underneath, but the melody stays the same. Sometimes the bassline plays an ostinato while the chords and melodies change.

The first time I ever remember taking notice of ostinato is in the beginning of the Smashing Pumpkins song "Today." The guitar riff starts out alone, then the band comes in. The chords change but the guitar riff never changes.

Activity:

Write a short melody. It can be as little as two notes. Then create a chord progression underneath it. It can help to write chords that contain at least some of the notes from the melody. See if you can come up with a few chords that sound good with the repeating melody.

Takeaway:

I find the ostinato often gives a song a feeling of persistence and determination. The melody stays steady and strong even when the chords are changing. Sometimes it's helpful to alter a note here and there in your ostinato phrase to fit the chords. Follow your ear!

Day 79: Add a Pedal Point

A Pedal Point is a sustained note that doesn't change as the harmony and chords around it change. It's almost like a one-note ostinato. Often Pedal Points happen in the bass, but they can happen anywhere.

Activity:

Use the chords and ostinato you created yesterday. Try to add a Pedal Point. Experiment with keeping the bass on a signal note (often the root note). If that doesn't work, try a sustained high note.

Takeaway:

The Pedal Point creates a sort of solid ground as other elements move around it. It's very common in strings on film scores when they are building tension.

Day 80: Chorus Prompts

Keppie Coutts is an excellent songwriting teacher. I had her on the Music Production Podcast and learned a lot: https://brianfunk.com/blog/keppie-coutts

Watch the portion of this video about writing choruses where she discusses Chorus Prompts (I highly recommend the entire video, but this link is cued up for you): https://youtu.be/oY81lrYs4nk?t=193

Here are the chorus prompts (reproduced with Keppie's permission):

So I realised...
So I decided...
So I'm going to...
That's why I always say...
What I really need to tell you is...
I'm so scared that...
What I most want to happen is...
What I need to know right now is...(phrase as a question)
You make me feel....

If I am a _____, then you are a _____

Activity:

Spend some time writing answers to these prompts. See if any of them inspire lyrics or song ideas. If so, pursue them!

These prompts are great "answers" to problems raised in a verse. You might use these to flesh out some older ideas you have for songs.

Takeaway:

Once you write your song lyrics, you can, of course, remove the prompts. Using the prompts helps give your chorus more of an impact. They will sound more like conclusions and thematic revelations. Be sure to spend some time with Keppie's work; she has tons of great songwriting ideas!

Day 81: Uneven Loop Lengths

Activity:

Create four new tracks. One track plays a 2 bar loop. On the next, a 3 bar loop. On the third, a 4 bar loop, and the fourth, a 5 bar loop. It can help to make the 3 and 5 bar loops percussive rather than melodic.

This would mean that the music would have to play for quite a while before it ever loops exactly the same way. Creating uneven loops is a great way to extend the life of a musical idea without it getting repetitive.

Takeaway:

Even subtle shifts in how our music interacts will help it stay fresh and exciting. I often have a 4 bar chord progression that will have 4 bar loops, 8 bar loops, 12 bar loops, etc. This way there are slightly different feelings each time the 4 bar progression repeats.

Day 82: Favoriting Some Sounds

Activity:

Many DAWs have some kind of "favoriting" feature in their browser, which allows you to identify presets and devices that you want to keep track of or categorize.

Spend a few minutes going through presets and plugins you want to have quick access to because you think you would like to use them in the future.

If you get inspired during the process, go with it! Inspiration is rare and fleeting. Act on it if it arrives!

Takeaway:

When it's time to make music, there's no better road block than trying to choose from thousands of presets. Setting aside a few presets you already know you like is a great time saver. I often find myself pretty excited when I go through my favorite sounds.

Day 83: An Album You Love

Activity:

Choose an album you love. Go through each song, and determine what the "Song Scenario" is for each song. Add these to your Reference File "Song Scenarios."

Takeaway:

Even though a song might be perfect for a particular situation, that doesn't mean more songs would be just as perfect! You can think of it as adding to a playlist of songs for that particular scenario!

Day 84: Your Favorite Time of Year

Activity:

In your notebook, brainstorm about your favorite time of year. Why do you love it? What activities are associated with that time? Go into detail about memories and possibilities. See if you can put together lyrics from the brainstorm about this time of year. If you put music to them, consider how the mood of the music might reflect the time.

Takeaway:

Writing about a time of the year can help us focus ideas and create themes for our songs. Plus, if you come up with a great song about a particular time of year, it might get played for that occasion every year!

Day 85: Opposing Emotions

Activity:

Today's activity is to write a song with opposing emotions. A happy sounding song with sad lyrics or a sad sounding song with happy lyrics. An aggressive song with gentle lyrics. Uplifting music with depressed lyrics. The possibilities are endless.

If these suggestions alone don't inspire any ideas, take a look at your Reference Files for inspiration (that's what they are there for!).

Takeaway:

We can play with different emotions when writing music. Using contrast between the lyrics and music can create all new feelings. For example, an angry lyric with happy music can create an interesting feeling of defiance with a touch of losing control. A love song lyric with dark music can sound a bit creepy or obsessive. Experiment with the emotional content of your music and lyrics and how they interact.

Day 86: A Distant Happening

Activity:

Turn on a television or radio station in a room adjacent to where you are. Try to find something with as little music as possible. If that isn't possible, a nearby conversation will work. Record whatever you settle on from a distance, like the next room. The point is to capture the chatter but not the specifics. We don't really want to hear what is said, just that something is being said.

Tip: it might help to eq away some of the lower bass frequencies. Often that's where a lot of rumble occurs, and that will only cover up the rest of the music we are about to make. For stuff like this, I find I can place a high pass filter anywhere from 100 Hz to 500 Hz without losing too much of the talking.

Now start creating music with this noise in the background. Notice how the emotion of the music you make affects how the background talking is perceived.

Takeaway:

When we are making music, we are creating a world for the listener to inhabit. I find that I can further transport the listener with recordings of natural sounds around me. Indiscernible voices are especially effective. Notice how the emotion of the music affects how the voices are perceived.

Day 87: What Not To Do

Activity:

Find a popular song that you don't like. Write down what it is you don't like about it in your notebook. Write down anything that you like about the song. List some things the song could do to make you like it more.

If you come up with any good ideas from this analysis, add them to your Reference File "Techniques to Try in a Song." Now see if you can make a song with any of those ideas, as well as some of the things you wrote down that would make you like the song more.

Takeaway:

We often learn a lot by thinking about what not to do. Dissecting what it is about a song you don't like can help you find the things you do like. Thinking about music you don't like in terms of what could be done to improve it will help you develop your own sense of style and taste. It's a great way to turn your annoyance into something productive!

Day 88: Do What You Don't Like

Activity:

Look back at yesterday's notes you took about the things you dislike about a song you don't like. Pick any one of those elements and try to write some music using it yourself.

Takeaway:

There's a lot of reasons why this exercise can be helpful. It forces you to work with something you don't like. This is bound to happen if you ever collaborate with or work for others. Learning to roll with ideas you don't love will help you maintain good relationships. It will challenge you to make lemonade with lemons. And this is good practice for when things don't go as we hope.

You are also now looking for techniques to improve the idea. This is what we do every time we produce, except this time we aren't leaning on something we already enjoy.

Lastly, it might give you a new perspective on that aspect of the song and show you its value. Maybe you don't like the context of the song it came from, but you might find you like this particular aspect in your music once in a while.

Day 89: Emulate an Influence

Activity:

Choose one of your favorite musical influences. Determine what one of their musical trademarks is. Without worrying about whether you are copying them too much, start creating some music that incorporates that particular element.

Takeaway:

Sometimes the best way to understand why something works is to try it yourself. For this exercise, we are allowing ourselves to do something a favorite influence is known for. Embrace it like it was your own quality. Think of it like trying on a new type of jacket. Odds are it will sound different on you anyway. Who knows, maybe this quality will be a good fit for what you do!

Day 90: The Fake Out

Activity:

Think of an idea you have for a song. You might check your Reference Files for one. Try writing some lyrics that are the opposite of what you will really say. A nice structure for a song would be to set the listener up for the opposite during the verse (fake them out) and then hit them with what you really want to say in the chorus.

Takeaway:

One of my favorite examples of the fake out comes from "God Only Knows" by the Beach Boys.

"I may not always love you.
But as long as there are stars above you,
You never need to doubt it.
I'll make you so sure about it.

God only knows what I would be without you."

Often what makes a song great is some sort of twist or surprise. The fake out is a great way to make the listener think one thing is about to happen, but then another comes by surprise.

Day 91: Gravedigging

When inspiration is low, it can be nice to review some of our unfinished projects for ideas. You might find a beat, a melody, chord progression, or just a few sounds that you can use again in a new project. You might even realize that something you lost interest in or forgot about is worth putting some more time into.

Activity:

Spend a few minutes looking through your old projects. Specifically open the ones that make you say "What is this? I don't remember this one?" If the idea itself isn't exciting enough to keep working on, maybe there's a beat, melody, or building block you can use in a new project.

This help page from Ableton shows how you can merge Live Sets and drag and drop elements from a Live Set into your current Live Set: https://help.ableton.com/hc/en-us/articles/360001830524-Merging-Live-Sets

Takeaway:

I refer to my unfinished tracks as "The Graveyard of Unfinished Ideas." Every once in a while, I do a little "gravedigging." It's usually enough to get me excited to make music. I might try to finish the song or just reuse some part of it.

Here is a link about my process, including a download of some sounds I managed to rescue from an old project. If you aren't finding anything useful, download the sounds I recycled and use them in your own track! https://brianfunk.com/blog/2020/3/28/grave-digging-free-ableton-live-pack-193

Day 92: Object Writing

Object writing is when we freewrite around a specific object. Focus on the five senses. Delve into memories and associations. Personify the object. Give it desires and aspirations. Don't judge what you are writing. Feel free to wander away from the original object. If the pen stops moving, return to the original object and choose one of the five senses to focus on.

Activity:

Spend five minutes doing some object writing. Your object today is: a candle.

Once you have finished, look for any material that can be used for song ideas. Add these to your Song Titles and Song Scenarios Reference Files. Feel free to explore any interesting lines as song ideas or lyrics. Be on the lookout for lines that you might take out of the context of the original object. Applying the characteristics of one thing to a completely unrelated thing can be the basis for interesting metaphors in your writing.

Takeaway:

I like free-writing activities like this because they train us to create without judgment. Make sure you don't worry about the quality of what you are doing. If you feel embarrassed if someone would ever read it, I give you permission to throw it away. But only after you have found anything useful in there!

Day 93: Rewrite the Lyrics

Activity:

Pick a song you like with a nice vocal line. Your job is to rewrite the lyrics, using the same phrasing and rhythms. Think of it almost like Weird Al doing a parody, except your lyrics don't need to be silly. Change the subject matter as much as possible. You might even use the Object Writing activity from yesterday as your inspiration.

Takeaway:

This exercise is designed to get you to focus on how lyrics are structured. Pay attention to the number of syllables. Notice the patterns of rhyme and replicate them. Where lines are repeated, repeat your replacement lines. This will give you a good sense of how to put lyrics together, and hopefully give you some tricks to use in your writing.

Day 94: Put Music to Your Lyrics

Activity:

Write music for yesterday's rewritten lyrics. Change as much of the music as possible from the original song, though it could be helpful to keep a similar beat or tempo as the original song. Alter the mood. Change the key and the chords. We are really just using the lyrical phrasing and structure.

If you do it well, no one will ever know where you found your inspiration!

Takeaway:

This isn't about copying. Many poets wrote poems that followed strict rules about the number of lines and the number of syllables per line. We are borrowing the structure of other songs to make our own unique ones. This allows us to focus on the words and melodies without worrying too much about the structure and form.

Day 95: Try a New Scale

Activity:

Today let's try writing a little bit of music in an unfamiliar musical scale. Many DAWs allow you to choose the scale you are playing in. If not, there are a ton of them here: https://en.wikipedia.org/wiki/List_of_musical_scales_and_modes
Spend a minute getting a feel for the mood of the scale. Is it sad, happy, mysterious, uneasy, etc? With that mood in mind, try writing something in that scale. Embrace the character of the scale, even if it's outside your normal style and genre. I find it helps to imagine writing a scene for a film.

Takeaway:

Going into unfamiliar territory is a great way to learn how to use music to convey emotion. The trick is to allow the feelings and moods of the scale to come through. If you find yourself trying to twist a dark scale into something light and happy, it might be better to use the light and happy scale.

Day 96: Show Don't Tell

Activity:

In your notebook, describe something you did today without saying what it is. Focus only on the actual steps and descriptions of the actions. Sensory Imagery (descriptions using any of the five senses) are especially helpful here.

For example, if I am describing going into my locker before soccer practice I might write: "I sit down on the cold wooden bench and spin the dial automatically without thinking about the numbers I am turning towards. The metal door opens with a squeak and I am hit with the smell of months of hard work on the field."

The point is to create the feeling of activity by breaking it down into individual pieces.

Takeaway:

It's been taught to writers for ages: show don't tell. Usually it results in more captivating writing. We get absorbed in the details of the experience and a feeling of importance is created by paying close attention to those details. Compare these two descriptions of the same situation:

"She left."

"The door slammed and the sound of her heels died away. I got up and put my ear to the door, as her car sped off into the distance."

The first one is just the facts. The second one has emotional power. In our music, we are usually going for the emotional power.

Showing not Telling can add emotional power and gravity to even the most mundane activities.

Day 97: Add Internal Commentary

Activity:

Go back to the Showing Not Telling exercise from yesterday. You should have a step-by-step description of some activity. Now add in some internal commentary. What are you thinking and feeling at each step of the way? Try to add importance to each action. See if you can weave back and forth from external events to internal thoughts and feelings.

Takeaway:

The actual events are only half the story. How we feel about them is just as important. Some internal commentary can drastically change how the events are perceived. You can use this to help support and add dimension to your lyrics.

It can be especially effective to set up the listener to expect one emotion but then surprise them with a different one using the internal commentary. I find this to be a great technique in the chorus of a song. Try spending a verse describing actions that might imply one particular emotion, then flip it in the chorus by going inside your thoughts and feelings.

For example, imagine my lines from yesterday's lesson are my verse:

"The door slammed and the sound of her heels died away. I got up and put my ear to the door, as her car sped off into the distance."

It feels sad. Notice the words "slammed" and "died."

But what if the chorus came in like this:

"I held back the urge to smile (internal commentary) as I ran to my phone to call my best friend. I told him to gather the boys and bring his guitar, as a weight drops from my shoulders (internal). Grab six-pack on the way, cuz tonight we're having a guys' night."

Suddenly I have the basis for a new hit country song called "Guys' Night."

Day 98: Verse, Chorus, Bridge or Situation, Theme, Outcome

One of the most popular song structures is the Verse, Chorus, Verse, Chorus, Bridge, Chorus form. Countless songs have been written using this or a similar structure (sometimes there's an instrumental after the bridge or even another verse).

I like to think of these sections like this:

Verse - The Situation: set the stage with time, place, characters, events, etc.
Chorus - The Theme: What is the message or lesson of the song?
Bridge- The Outcome: What happens after the events of the verses? How are we now that we learned the lesson of the Chorus?

Activity:

Using the writing you've done over the last two days, try writing a Verse, Chorus, and Bridge by thinking about them as Situation, Theme, and Outcome. Remember to incorporate both external and internal ideas in your writing.

Takeaway:

A song is a journey of sorts. Any journey worth going on has some element of adventure. That's what you are trying to supply by thinking about song structure in this manner.

Please remember, as is always the case with our 5-Minute Music Producer exercises: The point is to go through the exercises without judgment. Don't worry about how good any of the stuff you write is. That's all subjective anyway. It's about doing the exercise and building the muscle!

Day 99: Now Plan the Emotions (13 Musical Emotions)

Scientists have proposed that music covers 13 different emotions. You can read about it here: https://news.berkeley.edu/2020/01/06/music-evokes-13-emotions/

I also did a Music Production Podcast on this topic: https://brianfunk.com/blog/2020/2/6/what-is-your-listener-doing-and-13-musical-emotions-music-production-podcast-151

The 13 emotions they identified are: Amusement, Joy, Eroticism, Beauty, Relaxation, Sadness, Dreaminess, Triumph, Anxiety, Scariness, Annoyance, Defiance, and Feeling Pumped Up.

Activity:

Looking back on what we've written over the past few days, let's plan the emotion of each section of our song.

How should the verses feel? How should the chorus feel? How should the bridge feel?

We are just looking at our lyrics and applying any of these feelings to each section. Write down some ideas on how you think you could create those emotions. What type of instrumentation would each section have? Major or Minor key (or something else)? What kind of energy level?

Takeaway:

Whether there are actually 13 musical emotions is probably debatable. I often feel like music hits on emotions we don't really have words for. But we are not here to debate the science, we are just using it to help us write songs! Having an idea about the emotional arc of our song and how we might get there can make the path to getting there much clearer!

Day 100: Let's Make the Music!

Activity:

Now that we've planned out our song, let's put some music to it. Use your notes from the last few days as a guide. Don't feel completely stuck to it. If you come across something surprising that works, go with it!

Try working section by section. You can worry about the connective tissue between parts later. For now, we are just trying to come up with music that fits the emotions we are trying to convey in our song.

Takeaway:

Songwriters are always asked "What comes first? Lyrics or Music?" In the last few days, we started with lyrics and emotion. You may be the type that prefers to start with the music. I usually am. But mixing it up allows me to create in new ways. Always keep an open mind to changing aspects of your process. Every once in a while you may find an approach that helps you break out of old patterns!

Day 101: What's in the Fridge?

Activity:

Make music with a refrigerator! Collect sounds from a refrigerator. Does it hum? Open and shut the door. Capture the creaking and squeaking sounds. Open and shut drawers. Tap things that make noise.

Trim the audio files and arrange them into a beat or put them together in a Drum Rack. Feel free to change their pitches and time-stretch them. Now make a few 1 bar loops with them.

Takeaway:

Our everyday activities can yield interesting sounds. Capture the sounds and turn them into music.

Day 102: Let's Roll the Dice

Activity:

Go to Google's "Roll Dice" page: https://g.co/kgs/M1Hfzc

Choose the 8-sided Die. (You can use a real die if you have one)

Roll 3 times.

Use these numbers to create a chord progression in a key of your choice. For example, if I rolled 2, 4, and 6, in the key of C major, this would translate to D minor, F major, and A minor.

Takeaway:

Think of this as a challenge. You've been hired by a songwriting agency and your job is to write music using those chords. What will you come up with?!

Day 103: What's Happening Is...

Read this article: https://www.artofmanliness.com/character/behavior/sunday-firesides-whats-happening-is/

Notice the anaphora (The repetition of the first few words of a phrase. This article repeats the phrase "What's happening is."). This is a great technique for lyric writing!

Activity:

Today we will write lyrics to a song called "What's Happening." The subject matter is entirely up to you. The only rule is every line must start with the phrase "What's Happening…" (notice how these two words can be the start of either a statement or a question).

The more you write the better! Don't judge, just write!

Takeaway:

This is an exercise in anaphora. Anaphora creates expectation and predictability, which is an important key in writing catchy lyrics. Even though the phrase "What's Happening" is used throughout the article above, we can still use it to create original material. I think this is an important thing to remember. We can borrow small, inconsequential portions of other works to make our own.

Day 104: Another Ostinato

Ostinato is a musical phrase that repeats. Usually the chords or bassline will change underneath, but the melody stays the same. Sometimes the bassline plays an ostinato while the chords and melodies change.

The theme to the show Stranger Things uses an ostinato, which outlines a major 7 chord. Underneath, the bass hits two different chords, changing the emotion of that ostinato.

Activity:

Write a short melody. It can be as little as two notes. Then create a chord progression underneath it. It can help to write chords that contain at least some of the notes from the melody. See if you can come up with a few chords that sound good with the repeating melody.

Takeaway:

Ostinatos are fun because the emotion of the repeated melody changes as the rest of the music changes. Even though the ostinato is playing the same notes, it feels different every time the chords change.

Day 105: The Number One Song

It's time to do a little research on hit songs.

Activity:

Look up what the number one song in your area is. Listen to it and make a list of things you notice about it while listening. See if there are any ideas you can borrow. Add any ideas to your Reference Files (Song Scenarios, Chord Progressions, Song Titles, Techniques to try in a song).

Takeaway:

As you can see, this is a great exercise to revisit from time to time. The musical landscape is always changing. That means there is always new inspiration to draw from.

Day 106: 30-Second Song

Activity:

Choose one of your Song Titles from your Reference Files. Write a 30 second long song with that title. Give the song two different parts. You might think about the first part as introducing a problem and the second part as the solution. Tension then release. Either way, make sure there are at least two sections rather than just a 30 second loop.

Takeaway:

I like this exercise because it forces you to get straight to the point. You might find yourself doing unusual things like a 1-bar introduction instead of a 16-bar one. You'll be forced to distill the idea into its most pure form. Additionally, the idea of making 30-seconds of music is much less daunting than a much longer piece of music. Of course, you can always decide to make the song longer after you finish the exercise!

Day 107: Steal a Problem

Activity:

Think about a problem someone else has. It doesn't matter if you know the person or not. They might even be a character in a book or movie.

Imagine you had that person's problem and write about it in your notebook. What would it be like? How would your daily life be different? What would you be grateful for in your own life? What would you wish for?

Look for any interesting lyrics, song titles, or song scenarios and add them to the appropriate Reference Files.

Takeaway:

A myth about artists is that they need to suffer. You can tap into great song and lyric ideas through the experiences of others.

Day 108: Create the Emotion

Activity:

Thinking back to what you wrote about yesterday in the Steal a Problem exercise, what kinds of emotions were you writing about? Today, try to create some music that fits those moods. Consider using different sections of the song to communicate different emotions. There might be one that feels helpless and lost, while the next is determined and motivated.

Takeaway:

The most important thing we must do with our music is convey emotion. Practicing being deliberate about the emotion before we start writing can help us become more effective as producers.

Day 109: Create Some Lyrics

Activity:

Building on our Steal a Problem activity, let's try to write some lyrical content. Let's think in terms of two sections: verse and chorus.

Try making the first section about the problem. Go into detail about what life is like. Set the stage. Remember to be specific! Saying "I'm so sad" is much less effective than "I dried eyes before entering the door."

The next section can be thought of as the result of everything you set up in the verse. I like to consider the terms "therefore" and "but." Something happened in the verse, therefore… Something happened in the verse, but…" There should be some connection between the two sections. Consider the emotion you laid out in the verse and decide if the chorus is going to expand upon it (therefore…) or surprise the listener (but…)

Takeaway:

I find it helps my writing a lot to think of the relationship between the different sections. Ask yourself "what is the job of this part of the song?" Is it setting the mood? Building tension? Creating release? Surprising the listener?

See if you can avoid connecting with "and then…" It should be more like "this happened, therefore that happened" or "this happened but that happened." A song that goes "this happened and that happened and this happened" lacks a narrative arc. It's just a series of events. Make your sections have impact!

Day 110: Get Moving!

Activity:

Today, make some music while standing up. Put on a guitar strap. Set your gear up on at table you can stand in front of. Allow yourself to dance and move while you play and create. Focus on how the music moves you. You don't necessarily have to make dance music, but try to make something with a strong beat. The only goal today is to make music that will move your body.

Takeaway:

Check out this Ableton One Thing video from Daedulus: https://youtu.be/09m2yLf13b4

While Deadulus isn't always standing, he makes a great point about feeling the music. Sometimes sitting in a seat hunched over gear or a laptop is too passive and relaxed for the vibe you are going for. Getting the body moving and the blood flowing can help bring your energy level up so that you are excited about making music.

When I first started building a live performance set in Ableton Live, my first breakthrough was getting a DJ table that was adjustable up to countertop height. First, it gave me a limited amount of space for my gear, which forced me to make creative decisions about what my setup would contain (it all had to fit on the table). But most importantly it allowed me to move around while making music. When I got stuck, I would let the music play and simply feel it in my body. I found I was able to simply enjoy the music instead of staying in a critical and analytic mindset. I would literally "shake it out." Additionally, since the kindest thing a person could call my dancing is "silly," moving around helps me not take the process so seriously. It allows me to let go and have fun.

So close the blinds if you have to and lock the door, and get up and move to your music!

Day 111: The Challenge is Part of It

Activity:

Today's activity is more of a philosophical reminder: Part of making music *is* the challenge. It's not easy for anyone. Even professionals with proven track records struggle while making music.

On the Music Production Podcast, I've spoken to all kinds of people at every level of the music industry. None of them have ever said making music is easy. We all go through technical issues and self-doubt during the process. Since I started making music as a kid, I've always thought I'd have it figured out once I got to the next level. Every time I got there, I realized there are more problems to solve. And sometimes, reaching the next level has made me keenly aware of just how much I don't know and how much I still need to learn.

Today when you are making music. Pay close attention to when your mind starts to drift into these thoughts. Remind yourself that this is normal. It's part of the process. Recognize it is happening, then remember that every one of your favorite artists has been here too. They may even be feeling it right now as they work! Sometimes I like to picture my favorite artists struggling to find the right chord or crumpling up lyrics and tossing them in the garbage. The struggle is universal. The challenge is what makes it worth it. If it was easy then it wouldn't be special.

Takeaway:

We have to be prepared for the technical, mental, and emotional challenges that will come our way while making music. It's completely normal. It's like a boss in a video game. The bosses are what make the game exciting. The next time you face some sort of "boss" in your music making, remind yourself that this is part of the fun. Keep pushing through and embrace the challenges. They will make you stronger.

Day 112: Change the Theme

Many songs have similar titles. For example, both Radiohead and TLC have a song titled "Creep." They may have the same title but they have completely different subject matters and themes. This means we can reuse or alter the titles of songs we love, as long as we change the theme and perspective in our song.

Activity:

Browse through song titles in your record collection, CD collection, or your favorite streaming service. Write down any titles you particularly like. You don't have to be familiar with the song. Avoid any titles that are too specific (for example: "Sergeant Pepper's Lonely Hearts Club Band," "Piano Man," "Smells Like Teen Spirit," etc. The titles are either too iconic or too unique and specific to the artists that wrote them). When your list gets to 10 titles stop.

Pick one title that captures your imagination. If you are familiar with the song, come up with a different interpretation of the title. Now start writing your own lyrics around the borrowed title with a different theme. For example, I could also write a song "Creep," but mine could be warning someone to stay away from that "creep."

If you are not familiar with the song, then simply start imagining what a song with that title would be about.

Takeaway:

It's inevitable that we will write songs with titles that have been used before. That's not a problem if the song itself has a different meaning. Try repurposing titles you like. Remember, you can only really get away with this using titles that aren't completely unique.

Day 113: Create a Musical Mood

Activity:

Building on yesterday's activity of repurposing a title with a different theme and perspective, start making music that complements the emotions of your new song.

Feel free to use the original song you borrowed the title from as a reference of what not to do. Our goal is to keep the only similarity between the two songs in the title. Otherwise, our mood and theme should be different.

Takeaway:

This exercise can help strengthen your ability to create moods and emotions in your music. In yesterday's activity, we have determined the theme of our new song, today we are trying to support that theme musically.

Day 114: Inspiration from a Famous Speech

Activity:

Let's look for lyrical ideas and song titles from famous speeches.

This link has 35 great speeches from history: https://www.artofmanliness.com/character/knowledge-of-men/the-35-greatest-speeches-in-history/

Choose a speech and look for phrases that grab your attention. Add any that you think could make interesting song titles to your Reference File "Song Titles."

Takeaway:

The most memorable speeches contain wisdom, inspiration, and clever use of language. We can borrow some of those ideas for our own songs.

Day 115: Change the Roles

Activity:

Compose a short piece of music by changing the roles of preset sounds. For example, most plug-ins have preset categories for things like Bass, Lead, Pad, Percussion, etc. Try choosing a bass sound for your lead, or a pad sound for your bass. Try to use the sounds in ways they weren't intended to be used.

Takeaway:

Sounds designed to be used in one way can be quite interesting in other ways. As I design sounds and presets, I sometimes find it hard to categorize them. Even though I may have started with one particular intention, I find I get interesting and unexpected results when I attempt to do something different with them. This exercise is a great reminder that sometimes nice things happen when we use our tools in ways they weren't intended to be used.

Day 116: Let the Rhyme Do the Talking

Activity:

If you have one, get your Rhyming Dictionary or go to https://www.rhymer.com, which is an online one. Choose a word and find four rhymes for it. If you can't think of a word, here's one: Time.

In your notebook, do a few minutes of freewriting. Incorporate those four rhyming words into your freewrite. You don't have to worry about any kind of rhythm to your writing; just write continuously.

After you have written for a couple minutes and incorporated those four words, choose a word from what you have written and put that word into the rhyming dictionary. Repeat the process.

You can do this as many times as you want.

Once you are done, review what you have written for any interesting ideas for songs and lyrics. Add any ideas you get to your Reference Files.

The benefit of using words that rhyme to jumpstart this activity is that if you want to turn what you've written into lyrics you already have some rhymes to work with!

Takeaway:

Sometimes a great way to get ideas is to simply write around a particular topic. Just let the mind wander on the paper. You might be surprised at what you get!

Day 117: Simply Enjoy the Music

Activity:

Grab your instrument or load one up in your DAW. Make some music without recording anything. Just play. Let the music exist in the moment and then be gone. Take away the pressure of having to come up with ideas and capture them. Experience the pleasure of simply listening to the sounds.

Takeaway:

Long before music became a commodity or an occupation, it simply existed in the moment as was gone. You had to be there. It was a moment in time and then it passed.

These days we are constantly recording and capturing. We are thinking about producing and releasing. Countless hours are spent promoting it and sharing it. In some ways I think this takes away a bit of the magic. It can cause us to feel stressed out about the very thing we love.

For five minutes today, just spend some time enjoying the nature of the sounds you make. Let them happen and fade away. Don't allow yourself to worry about anything. Be present in the moment and appreciate the music for what it is while it lasts.

Day 118: What is the Song's Job?

Activity:

Pick a song that is important to you.

In your notebook, consider the following questions about this song:

- Is there a problem or conflict in the song? What is it?
- Is a solution offered to the problem? What is it?
- What type of mood are you in when you want to hear this song?
- How does the song change you and how you feel?
- What elements of the song help create this change?
- What activity would you want to be doing while listening to this song?
- Describe a time when this song would not fit the mood.
- Do you notice any changes in the tone/mood during the different sections?

Review your answers. Look for ideas you could use in your own song. Add them to your Reference Files. You might find some good Song Scenarios or Titles in your writing. There might be some Techniques to Try for a song of your own. Use them in your own songs!

Takeaway:

Learning from our favorite songs is a key to growing as a musician and songwriter. When something affects us emotionally, we should take note of it and try to understand what happened to cause that feeling. These are now ideas we can employ in our own music.

Day 119: Three Titles

Activity:

Look up the names of movies currently playing in theaters. Choose three titles that could make interesting song titles. You don't need to know what the film is about, and it might even be helpful if you don't. You can alter the titles if you get a cool idea.

Add these titles to your Song Titles Reference File.

Next, in your notebook, write some notes on different aspects of each song title. What might this song be about? What type of mood does it have? What perspective is it told from? Who is the singer? What problems does he/she face? What are the potential solutions to those problems? In what kind of situation would a person want to listen to this song (before a party, while working out, etc.)? What kind of instruments should be used?

Takeaway:

It's good to try to visualize and imagine different aspects of a song. Having a clear picture of the main ideas and themes can help you make decisions while writing.

We can find titles anywhere, but a title doesn't always have enough to inspire us to write. We also need to understand the message and purpose of the song. Thinking of a song as a solution to a problem can help. "When I'm feeling sad, this song can help," "When I need to get pumped before a competition, this song gives me energy."

Day 120: Use This Sound

Activity:

Make some music using this sample: https://drive.google.com/file/d/1EDD6MxbSJO9BL7wIp_4uQzmGRKN_O8eW/view?usp=sharing

It's a recording of my nephew when he was about 11 years old. He is singing into a toy karaoke machine.

You can use the sample however you like. Try dropping it into a sampler and playing it melodically. Place it behind a beat you are working on. Reverse it. Pitch shift it. Time stretch it. See what you can do with it!

Takeaway:

Sometimes it's nice to be forced to make a sound work. This is one of those cases. It might take into directions you don't normally explore!

Day 121: Get Oblique Again

Brian Eno created a set of cards for creative inspiration called "Oblique Strategies." Each card has an abstract statement that is meant to be used to help inspire creativity.

Activity:

Visit the Oblique Strategies online here: http://stoney.sb.org/eno/oblique.html

Each time you load the page you will get a new "card."

Use the "card" you get to come up with some music. It will be up to you to interpret the meaning of the card and how to apply it. This might be a bit challenging, but be as creative as possible!

Takeaway:

This time when I went to the site I got "Be Dirty." My first instinct was to use distortion. I often use distortion as a guitar player, so I thought about putting it on a less likely instrument: my voice. I added an Auto-Tune effect before it and a little delay after. The result was like having a guitar sound come out of my mouth! Really interesting and expressive. I wasn't singing words, just making sounds.

The Oblique Strategies are very useful for coming up with ideas you wouldn't normally try!

Day 122: Review Our Reference Files

Activity:

We've been collecting ideas in our Reference Files for about 4 months now! Let's take some time to review what we have.

Go through and review your different Reference Files: Song Scenarios, Techniques to Try in a Song, Song Titles and Lyric Ideas, Chord Progressions.

Look for anything that catches your attention. Pick one item from each of the lists and use them as a starting point for a musical idea.

For example, going through mine, I picked the following:

Song Scenario - The moment I decide to make a major life change

Techniques to Try in a Song - a steady increase in energy throughout the song (like Roy Orbison's "Crying"

Song Titles - "Never Again"

Chord Progressions - IV-V and vi, IV, V, I

Takeaway:

By going through this process I have a palette of colors to paint with. I have limited myself from infinite options and now have some creative restrictions.

Of course, if I need to veer away from any of these restrictions, I am free to. But at least now I have direction.

See if you can make use of the wealth of information you have collected at this point and make something new with it!

Day 123: New Reference File: Philosophies to Keep in Mind

Activity:

Today we will make a 5th Reference File called "Philosophies to Keep in Mind."

The point of this collection is to gather guiding principles that you can apply to your music. They could be workflow habits, policies, aesthetic decisions, mindsets, etc.

When you are ready to write music, refer to this list for some parameters to follow.

To help you understand, let me give selections from my own list:

- Inspiration doesn't have to be the first ingredient
- It should sound like a band's performance
- Pick it and go - Make a decision and move on
- Be 1 of 1 - embrace your weirdness, strengths, and weaknesses

- Verses- specific. Chorus - general/theme. Bridge - different perspective, twist, or after time passes
- Everything will be ok when you are ok with everything
- Don't get delight from things; Take delight in things. Find delight in taking delight in ordinary things
- Improv idea - "yes, and..." accept it and add to it. "Yes" creates momentum. "No" halts it.
- Songs are choices
- Make Strong Decisions
- Decide what it is not
- If you can't be grateful for what you've got you won't be grateful for what you get
- The story is key - what makes this human and real?
- There are no ordinary moments
- Perfect is the enemy of good
- Done is better than perfect
- focus on the work, not the outcome
- embrace the suck. The struggle is how we grow.
- slow is smooth, smooth is fast.
- wabi-sabi - the acceptance of transience and imperfection.

- Maintain Authenticity
- Encourage the Experimental and Unexpected
- Hit the page running
- Nothing is precious
- There is no time to waste
- Enough is a choice
- Let the seed idea germinate and flower, it might take a little time
- What's todays excuse? Tell it to f*ck off. Then get to work

Feel free to take any of these and add them to your list.

Takeaway:

Don't try follow every philosophy every time. Some philosophies contradict others. That's ok. Just pick a few that work with your ideas or mood. Sometimes you might decide to deliberately do the opposite. That's fine too!

In recording my band over the last year, I kept in mind "It should sound like a band's live performance." This philosophy alone helped guide me throughout the project. Could I have done some cool vocal chops, reversed guitars, and crazy spaceship noises? Of course, but that would have taken away from the unifying philosophy of the album. It helped me make mixing decisions about where to place elements in the stereo field so it sounded like you were in the room with the band.

Think about the philosophic approaches to making your music and look for these principles in the music you love. It will help you move forward and it makes difficult decisions easier to make.

Day 124: Avoiding Adverbs

Activity:

Adverbs are words that describe a verb. Often they end in "ly."

Examples: He walked quickly. She walks quietly. They walk lazily.

Often adverbs are a sign of lazy writing. There is usually a better verb or another way to describe the action that captures more emotion. Since we want to maximize emotional impact with our lyrics, avoiding adverbs generally creates better lyrics.

Better Examples: He scurried. She tip-toes. They drag their feet.

These examples are more interesting, create more emotion, and leave you more room in your lyrics for additional details to build your song with.

Take a look at some of your lyrics and see if you can find better verbs or phrases for your adverbs.

Takeaway:

We only have a limited amount of lines and time for our lyrics. It's important we cram as much as possible into each line.

When teaching lyric and poetry writing to my students I use the analogy of living spaces.

Writing in prose is like having a mansion to fill up and decorate. You can get all kinds of knick-knacks and furniture to fill the vast space.

Lyric and poetry writing is more like decorating a studio apartment; every inch counts. You have to maximize the space because there isn't much of it.

Treat your lyrics the same way. Scrutinize every word. If you can say it one line instead of four, that gives you three extra lines to further develop your idea.

Day 125: Use Filler Words for Rhythmic Purposes

Activity:

Yesterday I told you to ruthlessly cut out words you don't need and to use stronger verbs in place of adverbs.

Today I want to say the opposite.

Sometimes you can add a few filler words to help create rhythm to your lyrics to help convey the emotion of the vocal.

Throwing in a "Really" or a "very" or "doncha know that I'm" or a few extra "so"s can help propel a lyric rhythmically and add emotion.

I think the best person to listen to in this regard (and many others) is Michael Jackson. If you listen closely (Google his a capellas) he almost never stops making sounds. He is even known for iconic nonsense words "Sha-mon!" "Woooo!" "Yee-hee!" Sometimes nonsense words and sounds are more effective than real ones.

Review any of your lyrics. If you have a line that isn't working or needs extra emotional impact, you might not need to rewrite it, you might need to consider how it is delivered.

Takeaway:

Since lyrics are meant to be heard, it's just as important to think about the delivery as it is the words themselves. Listen to how your favorite artists deliver their lyrics. Pay attention to when they are using filler words and nonsense sounds to propel the rhythm and emotion of the song.

Day 126: A Roll of the Dice

Activity:

Go to Google's "Roll Dice" page: https://g.co/kgs/M1Hfzc

Choose the 8-sided Die. (You can use a real die if you have one)

Roll 4 times.

Use these numbers to create a chord progression in a key of your choice. For example, if I rolled 3, 5, 2, and 8, in the key of C major, this would translate to E minor, G major, D minor, and C major.

Takeaway:

Chance can be your friend. One reason is that you don't have to worry about making the decision. You just have to make the results work.

Day 127: Fill in the Next Section

Activity:

Yesterday you came up with a chord progression using the randomness of dice rolling. Today let's make a new section using the numbers you didn't roll.

I rolled a 3, 5, 2, and 8 yesterday. Today let's pick the 4 numbers I didn't roll: 1, 4, 6, 7. We can use these numbers to come up with chords for our next section. I'm going to leave out the 1 because that is the same as the 8, which I used yesterday. Staying in the key of C major gives me: F major, A minor, and B diminished.

Takeaway:

When we are writing different sections of our songs, we want contrast. Otherwise, the listener won't feel the change. One way to get contrast is to use different chords. I like to try some of the chords I haven't yet used in the key. If we look at the three chords I got today, we don't have the tonic chord of C major. The tonic chord feels like home. It's settled and stable. Leaving this chord out will create some tension. This is perfect for setting up either a new section that has the C major or a return to the previous section that also has the C major.

Day 128: The Sound of a Painting

Activity:

Choose a painting you love and create music to go with it. If you can't think of a painting, use "Starry Night" by Van Gogh.

Think about the mood and feeling of the painting. Consider what actions may be occurring. Imagine it as detailed as possible and use this to inform your musical decisions about tempo, tone, rhythm (or lack of), melody, scales, etc.

Takeaway:

A painting creates a world. That's the same thing we are trying to do with our music. We want to take our listeners into a world. Using a painting as inspiration can help give us ideas for the kind of world we want to bring listeners into.

Day 129: A Device You Never Learned

Activity:

Look inside your DAW's Browser for a plug-in you have not spent much time with. Make it a point to make something using that plug-in today.

I recommend recording the entire process of exploration with this plug-in. Often we do unusual things we wouldn't normally do once we understand how to use something properly. Take advantage of this beginner's mindset and record all of your experiments with the plug-in.

Takeaway:

Using a new piece of gear or software is a great way to break out of old habits. We are unable to turn to our predictable ways and we do things that are new and unexpected.

Day 130: Duplicate and Vary

Activity:

Program a 1 bar drum beat. Now double or duplicate that 1 bar loop but make a subtle change to the 2nd bar. Next, double or duplicate those 2 bars and make another change in the 4th bar.

Now choose a sound and program a 1 bar melody. Double or duplicate that melody and make a few changes in the 2nd bar. Double or duplicate those 2 bars and make an additional change in the 4th bar.

Continue this process a few times with additional instruments.

Takeaway:

In this exercise, we are making very small beats and melodies that have small changes every other bar. The point is to show how we can make bigger things by combining lots of smaller things.

I find it much easier to make 1 bar of music than to make 4. By making the original bar of music play for 4 bars with tiny changes we start to slowly build a composition. This can be a great way to get ideas going when we are stuck or feeling overwhelmed with possibilities.

Day 131: Use the News

Activity:

Let's have a look at the news for some potential song title ideas.

Scan your local newspaper or go to an online news source. Look for phrases that catch your attention. If you think any of them will be good song titles or lyric ideas, add them to your Reference File for Song Titles. See if you can find five potential titles.

Here are five I came across that you are welcome to use:

We Can't Lose
A Second Shot
Under Investigation
Navigating the Maze
Backstabbed in Return

Takeaway:

There are great titles all around, we just have to keep our eyes open. News articles are a great source because they are designed to catch a reader's attention and keep it.

Day 132: Give Your Title a Perspective

Activity:

Look back on your song title ideas that you found from news articles yesterday. Now try to imagine some kind of scenario. Who is involved in your song? What is the message? What is the problem?

From yesterday, I used "Under Investigation" and came up with this:

It's from the perspective of a person who did wrong once and is no longer trusted. They sincerely want to do better but have to regain trust. With everything they do, they are always "under investigation." They feel indignant and determined.

Takeaway:

Just having a title or line or two of lyrics isn't always enough. We have to flesh out the story a little and come up with an overall theme. Once we have that, it is much easier to make decisions about the elements of the song.

Day 133: Make Musical Decisions

Activity:

Building on the last two days of activities, start making some musical decisions. What is the mood of the song? What types of instruments would fit? Is there a song that has a similar emotional vibe? How do the sections of the song move the story forward?

Using the perspective for my title "Under Investigation," I came up with this:

Combination of electronic and rock band instrumentation, guitars/synths/acoustic and electronic drums. Similar emotion to The Police's "Truth Hurts Everybody."

Verses will have a brooding, tense feeling. Probably in a minor key. Choruses will sound more uplifted and determined, like the narrator will keep fighting even though they are always "under investigation." The chorus opens up and likely goes to the relative major key.

Takeaway:

I find that when I start to get a song idea, things don't really progress until some of these ideas are formed. Once they start coming together, the ideas come quickly and need to be captured. Writing these ideas down help guide the song and give it a clear direction.

Day 134: Blackout Poetry

Blackout poetry is a means of creating poetry from existing prose. To do it, find a piece of writing (a newspaper article, the page of a book, a magazine article) and circle interesting words and phrases. Then scribble out everything else with a marker. You are left with a set of words you found interesting. The activity is best with a physical piece of writing, but there is an online version that allows you to paste any text you want and click on the words you want to save: https://blackoutpoetry.glitch.me/#

Activity:

Find a newspaper article, a page of a book, or some other piece of text and circle any interesting words or phrases that catch your attention. If you don't have anything physical, find an online article and paste it into the link above.

After you have circled a number of words, scribble out the other words with a marker and take a look at what you have. What kind of emotions are present in the words? Does a story emerge? Record your thoughts in your notebook.

Takeaway:

Blackout poetry is a nice tool to turn to when inspiration is low. You don't have to come up with the material initially, you just have to filter it down. From there, you may find inspiration strikes.

Day 135: Flesh Out the Black Out

Activity:

Building off of your Blackout poetry exercise, attempt to flesh out the words you have "blacked out."

In your notebook, form sentences around words. Complete thoughts. Try to connect the words even loosely. Don't overthink it. Try to go with the first things that come to mind. You can always edit later. The point right now is to build up the material. The more the merrier!

Takeaway:

We are just trying to create material to work with right now. It's a collection phase. Get as much as you can. Try not to judge your ideas. And if you do, write down everything, even the bad ideas. At worst, the bad ideas will be reminders of where not to go with your writing. At best, you may look at the bad ideas in the future and not think they are so bad after all.

Day 136: Create a Narrative

Activity:

Take a look at your fleshed-out Blackout poetry from yesterday. Read it over and pay attention if any stories or memories pop to mind. As soon as something does, start writing it down. Continue reading and see if subsequent phrases and lines can be applied to what you have written today. Allow the story to go where the words take it.

Now write down the story of your fleshed-out Blackout poetry. Think about answer questions like who, what, when, where, and why. What is the conflict in the story? What do the characters want?

Takeaway:

Our minds evolved to recognize patterns. We are very good jumping to conclusions. An old friend doesn't say hello when we see them on the street. Suddenly, we create narratives about something we must have done to upset them, and we are filled with guilt and shame. In reality, maybe the sun was in their eyes and they couldn't see you! Use this tendency to develop your songs! Let your imagination run away with the idea without judgment.

Day 137: Build a Drum Kit

Activity:

Spend a little time compiling a Drum Kit you like. Search through your library of samples and plug-ins and find yourself a kick drum, snare drum, a closed high hat, and an open high hat, and two tom drums you like. Since drums have a huge impact on the energy of the song, consider whether you want a more mellow kit or one with higher energy.

Once you have your drum kit, save it as a preset for future use. When I name my presets, I always start it with my initials, BF. This way when I want to find my own sounds, I simply search for BF and I can see everything I have created.

Takeaway:

It's always good to have your tools on hand. Nothing can kill creativity faster than endlessly searching for the right sounds. Next time you need some drums for a track, go to the ones you have saved. Keep the inspiration going!

Day 138: Collect Your Tools

Activity:

Most DAWs allow you to tag "favorite" plug-ins and devices. Here's how to do it in Ableton Live: https://help.ableton.com/hc/en-us/articles/360000268570-Using-Collections-

Spend some time browsing through your collection of sounds and plug-ins and favorite any that you find inspiring.

In the Collections portion of my Ableton Live Browser, I have made categories for Drums, Instruments, and FX, among others. When I want sounds I know I love, I try presets from these Collections.

Takeaway:

Having the tools you love within reach is crucial to your workflow. Sometimes inspiration strikes suddenly. You want to be able to have the tools you love handy so you can act on it. It's so easy to lose inspiration while searching for the sounds to capture it. Have your favorite devices handy!

Day 139: Get Some Chords

Activity:

Google the chord progressions for three songs you love. You can usually find them by writing the artist's name, the song title, and chord progression.

Add the chords you find to your Reference File Chord Progressions.

Takeaway:

The same chord progressions get used in different songs all the time. It's helpful to have a database of progressions handy. You might even think about writing down an emotion next to the chord progression. I often like to pick a chord progression and try to make it work. I pretend as if I am collaborating with someone else who has brought this chord progression to our session.

Most of the time when I'm working, I know I can change any element of my song at any time. But making music is all about committing. This exercise helps me commit to a foundational aspect of writing a song, its chords.

Day 140: A TV Talk Show

Activity:

Create a short piece of music designed to be the theme song for a fictional daytime TV Talk Show.

Before you start, decide about the tone of this fictional show. Is it humorous? Laid back? Argumentative? Serious?

Try to create the mood with your song.

Make it no more than 45 seconds long.

Takeaway:

Sometimes we just need a specific prompt to get started. Once there is a purpose to my songwriting, everything comes much easier. Options and decisions are eliminated. The path becomes clear.

Pay attention to all of the music around you. Think about its purpose. Music made for commercials, television shows, and films, even customer service hold music, is carefully designed to create a feeling in the listener. Think about the emotions you want your listener to feel when you make musical decisions.

Day 141: Your Father's Name

Open the Musical Note Coder (Located at the end of this book).

Each letter of the alphabet has a corresponding musical note.

Activity:

Use your father's first name to come up with a collection of musical notes. These are the notes you are allowed to make music with today. What can you come up with?

Takeaway:

You can use the Musical Note Coder to give yourself a starting place for your music. It can be especially fun to code secret messages into your music!

Day 142: Recreate a Beat You Like

Activity:

Find a song you like that you listened to within the last week and spend five minutes trying to recreate the beat. You don't have to worry too much about the sounds themselves, just the pattern. Use this for the basis of today's music making, but take the rest of the music in an entirely different direction.

Takeaway:

It's ok if you don't get the beat exactly right. That's not the point. We are really just using this as a hack to get the momentum going. Do your best to do everything else in the song differently.

Day 143: Advanced Imagery - Double Nouns

We've discussed using sensory imagery in our writing (descriptions that use any of the five senses). Another way to build interesting descriptions is with double nouns.

Try using "Double Nouns" to convey your imagery. These are basically "Imagery Metaphors." They describe a sensation and make a comparison simultaneously. Examples: Concrete bed, a cat's sandpaper tongue, spiderweb hair, flagpole physique, leather skin, pumpkin head. Notice that these examples are two nouns (person, place, thing or idea) next to each other. They are very effective in creating an image, while not slowing down the story to give a description.

Activity:

In your notebook, write about a time you were uncomfortable. Pick a situation and write about it in detail. Think about the whos, whats, whens, and wheres of the situation.

After a few minutes, review what you wrote and look for opportunities to create Double Noun comparisons. Instead of saying "the floor felt like an iceberg," say "iceberg floor."

Takeaway:

This type of writing makes for interesting visuals in the reader/listener's mind. It's useful in songwriting because it takes up less space and leaves room for more lyrics. It can also allow you to find new rhythms for your lyrics to fit into. A lot of times these phrases make good titles.

Day 144: Chopped Lyrics

Activity:

Look at some of the things you have written in your notebook. On a separate piece of paper, write down any interesting phrases. Stop after you have about 10. Cut the phrases out with a pair of scissors and try to rearrange them to create some kind of logical order. Feel free to cut phrases in half and combine them with other phrases. See if you can come up with abstract lyrics this way.

Takeaway:

Many poets and lyricists create pieces by pulling lines from a variety of writings. They try to make some sort of sense of the lines, or at least put lines together that inspire thought. It's less about trying to tell a concrete story and more about leaving plenty of room for many different interpretations.

Day 145: 6 Word Memoirs

A 6 Word Memoir is an attempt to tell a story using only 6 words. As the story goes, Ernest Hemmingway was challenged to write a story in 6 words and he wrote, "For sale: Baby shoes, never worn."

Hemmingway's story is packed with possible interpretations. Maybe the baby died, maybe the baby was given up for adoption, maybe one of the parents took the baby away from the other, maybe the baby was born with giant feet…

The point is, the 6 Word Memoir forces you to squeeze meaning out of every word and piques the imagination.

For more information, listen to this NPR broadcast about 6 word memoirs. https://www.npr.org/player/embed/18768430/18775684

Activity:

Write a few 6 Word Memoirs of your own.

Here are a couple of my own:

I hope that they learned something. - Being a teacher, I end every day not really knowing if I really accomplished anything. None of my students look any smarter when they leave. If I were cleaning the floor or painting the wall, I could see the results of my work when I am done. As a teacher, it's hard to know if I did my job.

I wonder what that sounds like. - This one has to do with my love of manipulating sound. I love the adventure of putting sounds into samplers, reverse sounds, time stretching them, and running them through chains of effects. Every time is a surprise and every time is a learning experience.

Takeaway:

Writing a 6 Word Memoir can be a great way to start lyric writing. It forces you to focus on an idea. After you have the idea you can start fleshing out what it means and brainstorming additional ideas. One of the main causes of writer's block is not focusing and committing to an idea.

Day 146: Change a Chord Progression

Activity:

Find a song you love. Determine the chord progression. Add this chord progression to your Chord Progressions Reference Files. (You can usually find a song's chord progression by Googling the title and "chord progression").

Let's use this chord progression for our song, but first, we will make three changes.

- Change the order of the chords.
- Change the duration of at least one of the chords.
- Change the rhythmic pattern of the chord progression

Takeaway:

We don't need to reinvent the wheel! We can use ideas we already love as long as we make some changes to them. I've read interviews with artists I love who state they've written songs by changing songs they love until they are unrecognizable. This can be a great way to come up with your own songs or to simply experiment with other possibilities the original songwriter chose not to take.

Day 147: Take a Look Back

Activity:

If you're like many music producers, you probably have a collection of unfinished song ideas. Go through some of your unfinished ideas and pick the first one that sounds like it has potential.

Listen to it or play it. In your notebook, write down some things the song still needs. Maybe it needs a B section, more lyrics, a focal point, some kind of hook or melody.

Now that you have a list, try tackling these items one at a time. See if you can complete the idea. Try not to worry about how good it turns out, simply go through the process of finishing it systematically using your notes.

Takeaway:

Try not to feel much pressure in this activity. After all, if you weren't doing this, the song would still be gathering dust with the other unfinished ideas.

If for some reason (probably because you are being too judgmental!) you can't finish the track, make a list of all the things you like about the song and add those items to your Reference Files for Chord Progressions, Song Titles and Lyrics, Techniques to Try in a Song, Song Scenarios, etc. If nothing else, you can save the good ideas for a future project.

Day 148: Starts with the Letter R

Activity:

Try to make some music only using sounds, instruments, and presets that begin with the letter R. You can be a little creative about your interpretation of this rule. For example, you may use a Roland synthesizer or a red guitar. But try to keep within the limitation.

Takeaway:

The point of this activity is to create limitations. Having an endless ocean of choices is an easy way to get stuck. Narrow down your focus and the choices become easier to make.

Day 149: Random Word Generator

Activity:

Go to the Random Word Generator: https://randomwordgenerator.com

Take a few minutes to free-write about your word. Don't worry about any continuity between thoughts, meaning, rhyme, etc. Just write whatever comes to mind.

Once you are done, look for any interesting lines or topics. Add these to the appropriate Reference Files (probably Song Titles and Lyric Ideas and Song Scenarios).

Takeaway:

Focusing on a single word can be enough to get the imagination going. Making free associations can spur interesting ideas for songs.

I got the word "plagiarism." From this word I got a few lines I thought would work in a song.

"Took what wasn't yours"

"Lied about who you are"
"Made a fool of everyone"

These ideas might help get the ball rolling for a new song.

Day 150: 13 Musical Emotions

A study at UC Berkeley has found that music evokes 13 different emotions: https://news.berkeley.edu/2020/01/06/music-evokes-13-emotions/

The emotions are:

- Amused
- Annoyed
- Anxious and Tense
- Beauty
- Relaxing and Serene
- Dreaminess
- Energizing, Pump Up
- Eroticism
- Joyfulness
- Defiance
- Sadness, Depression
- Fear
- Triumphant and Heroic

I recorded a podcast that touches on these ideas: https://brianfunk.com/blog/2020/2/6/what-is-your-listener-doing-and-13-musical-emotions-music-production-podcast-151

Activity:

Add these emotions to your Reference List "Song Scenarios."

The next time you are writing your music and lyrics, pay attention to which emotions you are targeting. Think about ways you can evoke these emotions in your listener.

Takeaway:

One of the primary missions of music is emotional impact. A piece of music with no emotional impact is boring and meaningless. Make sure you are deliberate and intentional when you are creating your own music. Ask yourself whether what you are doing is adding to the emotional impact or not. If it isn't it might be distracting from it. Sometimes less is more!

Day 151: Borrowing Arrangements

When you break down the sections of a song, you may find its structure is surprisingly formulaic. We can study the way sections of songs we love are arranged and use that structure in our own music. This technique works especially well when we have a musical idea that we are having trouble finishing.

Activity:

Let's borrow the song structure of a song we love.

Find a song you love a drop it in your DAW. Figure out its BPM (often a Google search with the song title and "BPM" will give you a fairly accurate BPM).

Now place a marker in your DAW any time there is a significant change in the music. For example, the intro may go for 4 bars. Place a marker where it begins, then another where the first verse begins. Identify each section of the song to see how long each lasts. You might even place markers where interesting things happen within sections.

For example you can place a marker when the bass drops out during the second verse or extra vocal harmonies come in halfway through the chorus.

Once you have placed your markers, you can delete the song you borrowed from. Now you can start arranging your own track according to the markers you placed.

You might even consider saving the project with the markers in place as a template. You can then reuse this arrangement any time you are having trouble arranging a song.

Takeaway:

Song arrangements can be used and reused. Often songs from a genre have very similar structures. Pay attention to the conventions and use them as guidelines. You can and should deviate from the structure if the music calls for it. But getting the general structure down is a major step to finishing the song.

Here is a video I made about my method of "borrowing arrangements" in Ableton Live: https://brianfunk.com/blog/borrowed-arrangements-two-minute-ableton-live-tip-47

Day 152: External and Internal Details

We connect best with song lyrics that provide a balance between External and Internal details.

External details have to do with the world around us. We can best capture those using sensory imagery (descriptions that involve any of the 5 senses) in our writing.

Internal details are our thoughts, feelings, and reactions to the things that happen externally.

Seek to create a balance between external and internal details in your writing.

Activity:

Choose a Song Scenario from your Reference File. Spend a few minutes freewriting about it. Determine the whos, whats, whens, where, hows, and whys of the song.

Now review what you have and for every internal detail add an external detail, and vice versa. Come up with as much material as you can. Sometimes it helps to think of the external causing the internal and the internal causing the external.

From here you may have enough content to begin creating a song.

Takeaway:

The external details help set the scene of the song, while the internal details are where our revelations, lessons, and realizations happen. Creating a balance between external and internal details paints a fuller picture for the listener.

Day 153: A Double Ostinato

Ostinato is a musical phrase that repeats. Usually, the chords or bassline will change underneath, but the melody stays the same. Sometimes the bassline plays an ostinato while the chords and melodies change.

Activity:

Write a short melody. It can be as little as two notes. This is your first ostinato. Then create a chord progression underneath it. It can help to write chords that contain at least some of the notes from the melody. Now try to add another instrument that plays a different ostinato. So now you will have two different melodies that never change, playing over a set of changing chords.

Takeaway:

This can be tricky! I think it's best to keep things simple. Try doing two-note ostinatos over two chords to start. I also think it is helpful to have the second ostinato play its notes while the first ostinato is resting.

Day 154: Object Writing

Object writing is when we freewrite around a specific object. Focus on the five senses. Delve into memories and associations. Personify the object. Give it desires and aspirations. Don't judge what you are writing. Feel free to wander away from the original object. If the pen stops moving, return to the original object and choose one of the five senses to focus on.

Activity:

Spend five minutes doing some object writing. Your object today is: a key.

Once you have finished, look for any material that can be used for song ideas. Add these to your Song Titles and Song Scenarios Reference Files. Feel free to explore any interesting lines as song ideas or lyrics. Be on the lookout for lines that you might take out of the context of the original object. Applying the characteristics of one thing to a completely unrelated thing can be the basis for interesting metaphors in your writing.

Takeaway:

Remember to just write. Don't think about what goes down on the page, just get it there. Think of it like a contest: how much can you write today?

Day 155: The Number One Song

Activity:

Look up what the number one song in your area is. Listen to it and make a list of things you notice about it while listening. See if there are any ideas you can borrow. Add any ideas to your Reference Files (Song Scenarios, Chord Progressions, Song Titles, Techniques to try in a song).

Takeaway:

An important thing to keep in mind about number one songs is that they appeal to a very large audience. What are the things about this song that people like so much? Understanding this can help us with our own music.

Day 156: A Roll of the Dice

Activity:

Go to Google's "Roll Dice" page: https://g.co/kgs/M1Hfzc

Choose the 8-sided Die. (You can use a real die if you have one)

Roll 4 times.

Use these numbers to create a chord progression in a key of your choice. For example, if I rolled 3, 5, 2, and 8, in the key of C major, this would translate to E minor, G major, D minor, and C major.

Takeaway:

The roll of the dice is a fun and challenging exercise because it can be a great way to take you out of your normal patterns of choices. Make sure you take note of new ideas you come across. For example, if you enjoy your chord progression, add it to your Reference File Chord Progressions!

Day 157: Roll Again!

Let's continue our work from yesterday with a roll of the dice.

Activity:

Go to Google's "Roll Dice" page: https://g.co/kgs/M1Hfzc

Choose the 8-sided Die. (You can use a real die if you have one)

Roll 4 times.

Use these numbers to create a repeating melody. For example, if I rolled 2, 6, 4, and 8, in the key of C major, this would translate to the notes D, A, F, and C.

Create a melody using these notes. Play it over the chords you found from yesterday. Feel free to adjust any notes that don't feel right over your chords.

Takeaway:

Again, we are relying on chance. A lot of times the challenging part of making music is simply choosing a set of notes and chords from the practically infinite possibilities. Once we have some foundational elements we can begin creating music around those elements.

Day 158: Build a Beat

Activity:

Continuing with work on our chords and melodies from the last two days, let's add a beat.

Select a Drum Kit you like. Perhaps the custom kit you created on Day 137! Use that to create a beat for your chords and melody.

Takeaway:

Try to focus simply on progress. We are exercising the ability to move forward. It doesn't matter if you aren't working on the most amazing piece of music ever created at this point. What we are doing is improving our skills incrementally. We are showing up and working so we can invite the good ideas to materialize. They won't happen if we don't show up! And if we show up consistently enough and are prepared for them, we might eventually get something great!

Day 159: A New Location

Activity:

Find a new location to make your music today. If possible go outside (weather permitting of course). It might be a different room or another location completely. Maybe you try a coffee shop or visit a friend's house. Bring a simple setup. Keep it simple. See how working in a different place changes how you work.

Takeaway:

While I think it is important to have a dedicated space for working, changing that up once in a while can have a major impact. For one, you probably won't have your normal set of tools. This makes it harder to fall into predictable patterns. Additionally, you are exposed to different stimulus and that will change the way you think about your music.

My band is lucky enough to have two different locations to practice. Our main place is my house, and the other is our drummer's house. I've noticed a difference in myself when I'm not home. I don't worry about small things like letting my dogs out and feeding them. I get the benefit of leaving the house and getting fresh air. Since I simply use whatever amplifier our drummer has set up for the guitar, I focus less on my tone and gear and more on the notes I play. My overall approach to music is a little more adventurous and experimental.

Think of it as a small vacation. Have fun and see what happens!

Day 160: What Not To Do

Activity:

We often return to familiar patterns when making music. If we aren't careful all of our songs can start to sound the same.

Take some time to make a list of things you tend to do. Consider the keys you gravitate towards, the BPMs you use a lot (especially the default template when you open your DAW), instrument arrangements, presets, soft synths, instruments, song forms, effects, genres, etc.

Title this list "What Not To Do."

Use this list as a guide for your next music-making session or any time you start to feel like you are repeating yourself.

Takeaway:

We all get into routines and habits. Sometimes those are effective in helping us make music, but sometimes it results in songs that are a lot like all of our other songs. This can be a good thing and might help us develop our own sound, but every

once in a while we should break out of our ways.
It might lead to new discoveries!

Day 161: Try Another Medium

Activity:

The last few days we've been in the spirit of getting out of our usual habits. Let's try something new today.

Instead of making music, make a different kind of art. Draw a picture, take photographs, sculpt, knit, paint, whatever you think would be fun. We are not trying to create masterpieces, we are simply expressing ourselves in a different way.

Takeaway:

It can really help to think about different methods of expressing ourselves. We make new connections and come up with new ideas. Often this gives us new ways of thinking about our music.

Day 162: Put Your Art To Music

Activity:

Once you have some other piece of art from yesterday's exercise, use it as inspiration for some music. Think about what types of sounds a musical representation of your new art would have. What would the genre be? What would the lyrics be about? See if you can then make some music that complements the art you made yesterday.

Takeaway:

Many musicians find inspiration through other artistic mediums. They might be writing for a film or creating a soundtrack for a painting they love. By looking for inspiration in other art forms, we will start to come up with stories and meanings about the art that we can apply to our music. This gives us direction and helps us make musical decisions. Using our own art is great because that art can be used for album covers, videos, and other aspects of our releases.

Day 163: Use Your Chord Progressions

Activity:

Over the course of these daily exercises, we have accumulated a collection of Chord Progressions in our Reference Files. Choose a progression and use it as the basis of today's music-making activity. Experiment with them. Try different timings and rhythms.

As you play the chords, pay attention to the emotions they have. What is the overall feel of these chords? In what chords do you feel tension or release? Do you notice differences as you play each chord for different lengths of time? Think about how these feelings might reflect things we experience in life.

Takeaway:

Today we are making use of some of the ideas we have collected. It's good practice to put your ideas to work. It can be easy to always be collecting ideas but never using or finishing them. Make it a point to try to make the most of today's chord progression. There was a reason you wrote it down!

Day 164: Give it a Title

Activity:

Looking back on the chord progression you were working on yesterday, visit your Reference File for Song Titles and Lyric Ideas. Think about those emotions you were feeling with your chord progression and see if any of your titles fit those emotions. Write down any of the titles that work. You might consider alternate interpretations of the titles than originally planned when you wrote them down. For example, I originally wrote the title "Left Behind" thinking it had to do with a lover leaving me. But after thinking about the optimistic chords I had, it now fits the context of a person leaving home to start a new chapter in their life. Same "Left Behind" theme, but much different story and emotion.

Takeaway:

Our titles need an emotional context. When we communicate, the meaning of what we say depends largely upon our body language and tone of voice. Just think of how many different ways you could say "get over here." It could be playful, angry, excited, etc. It all depends on how we say it and what our body is doing. Our titles are similar. The music provides a lot of that context.

Day 165: The First Line

Activity:

The first line of a song is extremely important. This is where we can grab our listeners and make them want to hear what we have to say. If the first line isn't captivating, we might lose their attention.

Take a look at this list of great opening lines to novels: http://americanbookreview.org/100bestlines.asp

You might also look at opening lines in your favorite movies.

Pay attention to how the writers get the audience's attention. How do they create tension and curiosity?

Here are some techniques you can use to create interesting openings for your lyrics:
- Try being vague, create mystery by not immediately letting the reader know exactly what you are writing about…
- Try using vague words like "it" before explaining what "it" is.

- Start with dialogue. (Ever walk into a middle of a conversation and have to ask "what are you guys talking about?!")
- Start somewhere besides the beginning.
- Say something shocking.
- Start in the middle of the action.
- Make the reader question the narrator's credibility.
- Create a problem.

Takeaway:

First impressions are huge. In a world of ever shrinking attention spans, you need to grasp your listener's attention as soon as possible. Make sure the first line of your song create interest.

Keppie Coutts of *How to Write Songs* has an excellent video on first lines of songs: https://youtu.be/F6njy21wZoE

Day 166: What Can We Learn

Activity:

Let's add to our Reference File "Techniques to Try in a Song."

Think of a style of music you don't normally write.

Do a Google search for "How to write a (genre of your choice) song"

Try to find a few new techniques that you can add to your Reference File.

Takeaway:

I chose to Google "How to write a K-Pop song." It's not because I want to write K-Pop. I want to learn something from a different style of music. One tip I read was that the rhythmic stresses of a melody usually change between sections. A verse melody might focus on the downbeat, while the pre-chorus melody is more syncopated. This creates contrast and tension, which helps the chorus feel more satisfying when it returns to the downbeat emphasis.

These are not strict rules for the genre, they are simply conventions. And this particular convention would work in any genre of music. It helps create contrast between the different sections of the music while playing with the feelings of tension and release.

Studying different genres of music can help us add interest to the styles we normally like to write in.

Day 167: What and Why

Activity:

We are going to write about something that happened that you didn't like. It can be big or small, close to you or across the world. Get something in your mind and get your notebook.

Spend a couple minutes describing what happened. Who, what, when, where, how, etc.

Then write about what it was about the situation you didn't like. Now we are talking about the "why." Which of your principles were violated?

When you are done, look for any song titles or ideas.

Takeaway:

Often the verse of a song deals with the specifics of a situation. The chorus is usually the theme of the song. This writing activity can help you get those parts of the song together.

The first exercise is good for verse material. The details set the stage for the song.

The second exercise lends itself to chorus ideas. You are getting to the message of the song. You are telling the listener why the events of the verse are important.

Day 168: Much Faster Than Usual

Activity:

Today try to create some music at a much faster BPM than usual. Crank up your metronome and see what you can come up with at a tempo you are unaccustomed to.

Takeaway:

Sometimes our preferred genres box us into specific BPMs. Experimenting with different BPMs might unlock new ideas.

Day 169: Much Slower Than Usual

Activity:

Now we will try a much slower BPM than we are used to. Slow things down below what you are used to and see what comes of it.

Takeaway:

It never hurts to try something new. Slowing things down might help you explore new ways of creating.

Day 170: Change the Speed

Activity:

Look back on one of your ideas from the last two days, either the faster one or the slower one. Now experiment changing the time of that idea. Go in the opposite direction. Try making the slow piece a fast one and vice versa. See how the idea changes at different speeds.

Takeaway:

Sometimes a song works just as well or better at a much different tempo. Many artists have had success with covers of well-known songs by drastically changing its BPM. Experiment with your idea and see if changing the speed changes the feeling and meaning of the song.

Day 171: A New Place

Activity:

Relocate yourself to a place you don't ordinarily make music. It could be a different room, outdoors somewhere, a coffee shop, or any other place that is a little different than the norm. Try to use the fresh environment as inspiration for something new. Don't forget to check your Reference Files for ideas!

Takeaway:

New scenery can really change how our mind works. We have different thoughts and that leads to different ideas. Our energy levels might be different and our attitudes slightly shifted. Every once in a while I like to relocate and see if something fresh comes of it. Usually it does!

Day 172: A New Approach

Activity:

Pick some aspect of your normal workflow. Today, let's do something new.

Do you normally start with drums? Piano? Lyrics? A sample? Pick a different approach you are less familiar with. Try a different DAW. Work with a new piece of gear or software. Put yourself out of your comfort zone and see how it affects your creativity.

Takeaway:

I'm a big believer in having workflows we can turn to. After all, much of this course is about setting yourself up with strategies you can turn to.

But it's important not to underestimate the power of novelty. New approaches lead to new ideas. I come up with much different ideas when I start on a keyboard compared to when I pick up a guitar. Even programming drums is much different than playing them. I come up with different ideas, chords, and melodies. The energy I bring to the songwriting is different too.

Eventually, if we have a number of different ways to approach music production, we can change our approach when our normal ways aren't working. We can learn which approaches fit which situations.

Day 173: Song Topics

Activity:

Pick an album you love.
Look at the songs and in a few words, write down what each song is about. Add these to your Song Scenarios Reference File.

Here's what I got by doing the exercise (Feel free to add them to your list!):

Getting ready for a good time
Longing for someone you used to have
Finding someone who is a perfect match
Seeing Through Someone
Don't Stop
Putting up with someone no matter what
Saying Goodbye
Things not changing
Things are backwards

Takeaway:

This exercise is useful when the question "what should I write a song about" comes up. Look for interesting topics in other songs. Put your own perspective on it. The thing I like about keeping a list like this is after a short while, I no longer remember what songs gave me the idea. When I look at the list, my own ideas and interpretations of the topics come to mind, which are usually completely different from the song it came from.

Day 174: Get Lost

Activity:

Set up an instrument to play, whatever you like acoustic, electric, electronic, a plug-in, etc. Start recording and just play the instrument in an exploratory way. You aren't performing. It's more like noodling. Explore melodies and chord progressions. Make unusual sounds and noises.

If you are sticking to five minutes, stop recording after five minutes. Otherwise, feel free to play for as long as you like. Stop the recording and you are done!

Takeaway:

The point here is to forget you are recording and to get lost in the playing. Sometimes recording makes us nervous and uptight in our playing. Sometimes trying to write music makes us overly critical and judgmental. This exercise is designed to help you lose sight of those feelings and enjoy playing in the moment.

Day 175: A Nugget of Gold

Activity:

Listen back to your recording from yesterday. Keep in mind that you were playing in a sort of aimless and adventurous way, so don't judge it harshly!

Pay attention for any interesting moments. It might be a few minutes or even just a couple of seconds. Make a note of these moments. Place a marker there, write down the time, or cut it out from the rest of the playing.

See if you can make anything out of any of the moments you took note of.

Takeaway:

I especially like to use this method when I am using a new piece of gear or one I'm not that familiar with. This is also the main method by which I come up with vocal parts. I loop a section and record myself singing gibberish and nonsense over it for a little while. Every once in a while I find a vocal phrasing or melody I like. Sometimes I say something interesting or find the right combination of vowel and consonant sounds. When I listen back, I can find those spots and start developing the vocals around those moments.

Day 176: Start with a Pedal Point

A Pedal Point is a sustained note that doesn't change as the harmony and chords around it change. It's almost like a one-note ostinato. Often Pedal Points happen in the bass, but they can happen anywhere.

Activity:

Choose a key and create a pedal point bass with the root note. You can choose to have the bass line simply hold one long consistent note or you might create a rhythm using only that one note.

Now build a chord progression and beat on top of the pedal point. Start simply at first, perhaps with two chords. You can of course add chords if you like.

Takeaway:

A Pedal Point in the bass can help give us a foundation to write over. Depending on the material that plays on top of the bass Pedal Point, the sound can take on many different emotions.

Experiment with how the feeling of your music changes as you try different chords over the Pedal Point.

Day 177: Add a Melody

Activity:

Building on yesterday's pedal point activity, try writing a melody for your idea. Think about the melody in terms of shape. Your pedal point is like a straight line. Your chords will being moving around that straight line. What type of shape do you think would work well over them? Maybe a melody that moves up twice and then down once? Or perhaps a melody that goes down and then up on the last two notes? Experiment until you find something you like.

Takeaway:

Notice the way the notes of your melody push and pull against the pedal point in your bass. Pay attention to how you are creating either a sense of tension or release. The melody can often affect whether the pedal point feels stable and tonic or tense and in need of release.

Day 178: The Laundry List Song

Activity:

There are many styles of songwriting we can follow. One is the "Laundry List Song." It involves listing things in the verse and giving the punchline to those things in the chorus. Some good examples are Stevie Wonder's "I Just to Say I Love You" and Sam Cooke's "What a Wonderful World," a portion of which is below. In Cooke's song, the verses list things the singer doesn't know, while the chorus is the one thing he does know.

Verse

Don't know much about history

Don't know much biology

Don't know much about science book

Don't know much about the French I took

Chorus

But I do know that I love you

And I know that if you love me too

What a wonderful world this would be

Looking at your Song Titles Reference List, pick one song title and see if you can make it into a Laundry List song. Scribble down ideas in your notebook. Don't worry about whether your ideas are any good. Just try to come up with as many as possible. While you are at it, add "Laundry List Song" to your Techniques to Try in a Song Reference File.

Takeaway:

Adopting a style like the "Laundry List Song" helps pave the way for the entire song. Once you have decided what the list will be about and how the chorus responds to the list, the writing becomes much easier. The result is often a satisfying twist that makes the chorus feel important and memorable.

Day 179: Random Song on the Radio

Activity:

Get your notebook, put on a popular FM radio station, and listen to whatever song comes on next. Write down anything interesting about the song. Pay attention to its structure, its lyrical content, the instrumentation, etc. Take notes as fast as you can about as many elements as possible. You can write about how it makes you feel. Think about when a person might want to listen to this song. What is the production like? What do you like? What don't you like?

Once the song is over, you can stop writing. Take a look at your notes and see if you can use anything you've written as ideas for your own songs. Write down any ideas in the appropriate Reference Files so you will have them for later.

Takeaway:

Adopting a curiosity about music is a great way to learn to appreciate all types of music. Even if you don't like a song, figure out what is causing that emotional reaction in you. Music is all about communicating emotion, and we can learn a lot from how songs make us feel. Turning any listening experience into a learning experience will help you grow as a songwriter and music producer.

Day 180: An Uncommon Time Signature

Most popular music is created in 4/4 and 6/8 time.

Activity:

Today we will experiment with an uncommon time signature. Try something like 5/4 or 7/4. It helps to divide them in your mind. For example, you can think of 5/4 as a measure of 3 followed by a measure of 2.

Takeaway:

We are quite used to hearing music in 4/4. Using a different time signature, even just for a particular section of a song, can help keep things exciting and interesting. Changing the time signature can alter the mood and feeling of a track. Since 4/4 is very comfortable, try using it in a more stable part of a song, like the chorus. Then try an unusual time signature in the prechorus for a more unstable feeling that can highlight the prechorus' tension so the chorus can have a big release when it goes back to a stable, familiar structure.

Day 181: An Uncommon Scale

Activity:

Much of popular music is written in Major (Ionian) or Minor (Aeolian) scales. Today we are going to write in a different scale. If your tools allow you to select a scale, choose one you rarely use. Otherwise, you can Google exotic scales.

Here are the modes of major: https://en.wikipedia.org/wiki/Mode_(music)

And here are some more interesting ones from a LANDR blog post: https://blog.landr.com/7-weird-scales/

No need to go too crazy; just quickly choose something you don't ordinarily use and see what you can do with it.

Takeaway:

Pay attention to the emotions in the scales. If it doesn't sound like it would fit your style of music, consider what styles it would work in. Perhaps it might fit in a film score to capture certain moods.

When I was younger, I wrote off just about any scale that wasn't major, minor, or pentatonic. I figured I would never use them because they didn't fit the narrow style I was writing in. Now I realize that they can be useful for creating different types of moods within any genre I am writing. They become flavors you can add to your songs to give them new life.

Day 182: The Town You Grew Up In

Open the Musical Note Coder (Located at the end of this book).

Each letter of the alphabet has a corresponding musical note.

Activity:

Use the name of your hometown to come up with a set of notes to write music with. See what kind of music you can come up with. You might even make the song about your hometown.

Takeaway:

In a world of infinite options, it can be nice to have some choices made for us. The Musical Note Coder is a great way to let chance play a role in your writing!

Day 183: A New Section

It's a good time to review some of our unfinished projects for ideas!

Activity:

Open an unfinished project of yours. Today, we are going to try to make a new section of this song. The key is to work fast.

Take one element of the song and duplicate it. Now let's change it a bit to come up with a new part. If it's a beat, switch the beat up a little bit. Make it more exciting with extra parts. Change some of the accents. Make it a more mellow version. If it's a chord progression, try reversing the order of the chords. Start a new progression with the relative major or minor chord (To go from Major to Minor, go up down 3 steps. To go from Minor to Major go up 3 steps. Ex: G Major becomes E minor, A Minor becomes C Major.) Just make a couple of changes to the part and start adding new layers on top.

Takeaway:

Best case scenario, you might find new life in an old idea this way. Worst case scenario, you practice making a new section to a song. That will make you better at it the next time you have a great song idea!

Day 184: Freewriting on Change

Activity:

Spend some time today freewriting in your notebook about change. Maybe it's something you want to change or a change that has recently happened. Or maybe it's just the way that things all eventually change. Anything you like! And feel free to let your mind wander. The only rule is that you keep the pen moving for the full five minutes.

When you are done, add any interesting ideas to your Song Titles or Song Scenarios Reference Files.

Takeaway:

Spending a little time letting your mind wander is a great way to come up with new ideas for songs. Just allow your mind to hit the page. Don't judge your writing. Don't question it. This exercise is not meant to be a finished product. It's just a way to find new ideas.

Day 185: Get Some Rhymes

Activity:

If you have one, get your Rhyming Dictionary or go to https://www.rhymer.com, which is an online one.

Take a look at your freewriting on change from yesterday. Pick a key word and write it on the righthand side of the page. Then go through the rhyming dictionary and find three rhymes for the word. Write the rhymes on the righthand side of the page underneath the original word. Try to pick words that you think will make for interesting connections, but don't overthink it.

Now try to fill in the rest of the line before the words. Let the rhymes inform what you write.

Repeat this process with another key word from your freewrite.

Repeat the exercise until you have a bunch of lines. Think Quantity over Quality. We can worry about refining what we write later.

Takeaway:

Writing around the rhymes is a great way to get ideas flowing. You don't have to use exactly what you come up with, but you can use it to put ideas together. I like this method because it turns songwriting into puzzle solving. You already have some input, now you just have to connect the dots to make it work.

Day 186: What Are You Rhyming About?

Activity:

Let's build off of what we came up with yesterday with our Get Some Rhymes activity.

In your notebook, look at your lines and write about what the lines mean. Write in plain language what this song is going to be about. Forget about rhyming and lyrical beauty. What is the plot? Who are the characters? Who is singing the lyrics? Who are they singing to? When and where does the story take place? What are the conflicts? How are they resolved or how do the characters make peace with the conflicts?

Keep in mind that you are simply finding the meaning suggested by some of your rhymes. It doesn't all have to be in the rhymes you wrote. Use your imagination. Build a story around the rhymes you wrote yesterday.

Takeaway:

It can be very helpful to write out what our songs are about in normal prose. It helps us get a sense of what direction the idea is going. Our lyrics don't have to always explicitly state the meaning of the song. A little ambiguity in the lyrics allows listeners to interpret the song in their own way. By understanding the overall concept of our song, we can start making musical decisions that fit that idea.

Day 187: Refine the Rhymes

Activity:

Today we will continue to build on our ideas that we started a few days back when we did freewriting on change, found rhymes, and then wrote out the story of our song in normal prose.

Take a look at your rhymes from Day 185 and your plain language writing about the song idea from yesterday. Now let's start refining our rhymes and build our song lyrics.

Let's begin in the "more is better mindset." Take note of any aspect of the plain language writing that is not present in the rhymes. Try to incorporate that into your rhymes. Feel free to use a rhyming dictionary again, or just see what you can come up with on your own. If you think it, write it down. Don't be judgmental. Just try to fit some of the concepts about your song into the rhyming lines that you already have.

Here's a little challenge… try to focus on showing and not telling. Instead of telling us "she got upset" try showing us what happened, "her voice broke, she covered her mouth with her hand and turned away." The showing way is more powerful because it creates an image in our mind.

After you've added some lines to fill in the story, you can go into a more critical mindset. Look for anything you wrote that doesn't fit the idea and put it aside.

Takeaway:

If you notice, over the last few days we have done a little bouncing back and forth between looser freewriting and more crafted lyric writing. I find that both styles help the other. Once I exhaust my thoughts in one manner of writing, I switch to the other. Often my freewriting contains phrases and lines that can become part of the lyric writing, and the lyric writing helps create the details that help me form the overall concepts of the song.

Day 188: The Details and the Message

Activity:

Generally in songwriting, the verses set up the details and specifics of a situation (who, what, when, where). The choruses then deliver the message or the thematic ideas of the song (why, how, and "now what?!").

Take a look at your rhymes and lyrics from the last few days and separate them into the details about the story, which are the verses, and the more thematic lines into your chorus.

It may help to revisit the Chorus Prompts from Keppie Coutts of How to Write Songs. The Chorus Prompts are the connective tissue between your verses and choruses. You might actually include them in your lyrics or simply imply them:

So I realised...

So I decided...

So I'm going to...

That's why I always say...

What I really need to tell you is...

I'm so scared that...

What I most want to happen is...

What I need to know right now is...(phrase as a question)

You make me feel....

If I am a _____, then you are a _____

If you have lines that aren't quite setting the scene or delivering the message, those might make good bridge lyrics. The bridge often contains some type of twist or plot development. Maybe those lines will fit nicely here!

Takeaway:

Up until today, we were simply collecting ideas and rhyming lines. Now we are organizing them into a cohesive structure. The manner in which we construct and organize our lyrics can make all of the difference. Consider how the impact of your lyrics changes depending on where they occur in your song.

Day 189: Planning the Music

Over the last week or so of activities, we have focused on lyric writing first. The most common question songwriters get asked is if they write the music or lyrics first. There's no right way, and most songwriters do both. Sometimes they happen at the same time.

Today we will prepare ourselves to start writing the music... but first, one more activity!

Activity:

Looking at your lyrics lets plan how each section of our song should go musically. Get your notebook and write down some notes.

For the song as a whole:

What is the mood and vibe? Is it a positive or negative feeling? What type of chords and musical keys would fit these moods? How fast should it be? Does it have a frantic feel or a more laid-back one? Do you think a straight rhythm or something more syncopated would serve the song?

For the verse:

What type of mood is in the verse? Are there any lines you'd like to draw attention to? What type of instrumentation would fit? What is the energy level? Does the verse call for a melody that makes large jumps or stays relatively small? What kinds of chords do you imagine you'd use?

For the chorus:

Is there a change in mood from the verse? Are there any lines that capture the theme that should be repeated? How does the shape of the melody differ from the verse? How are the chord progressions different from the verse? Are they different?

You might also want to highlight any lyric that you think is especially important. Those lines might receive some type of melodic or instrumental ornamentation.

Takeaway:

In this step, we are thinking about how we want to color our lyrics. Generally, we want the musical ideas to fit with our lyrical ones. But sometimes an unexpected contrast can create very interesting moments. We are simply trying to plan how we want to frame our lyrics musically. This will make the next step of actually creating the music much easier.

Day 190: Let's Create the Music

Activity:

Now that we have planned and organized our ideas, it is time to start building the music.

Start however you like. You could choose something rhythmic or start with chords and melodies. I often like to start with a placeholder beat to play chords over. Pick one section and focus on that. You could start at the beginning or you might begin with the chorus. The choice is yours. If one approach isn't working, try another.

A word of advice… don't overthink it too much and don't take too long. Once you get close to the feelings you wrote about yesterday, move on. You can always make adjustments later, but the most important part of getting music finished is to commit. Once you have a sketch of an idea, you can then decide to edit and refine. For now, let's just get the most basic elements in place.

Takeaway:

Keep the spirit of moving forward in this part of the process. Don't worry about getting things perfect. Get something down and later we can try to perfect it. You can't edit what you don't have. Try not to worry about how it comes out as much as just getting through the process.

Day 191: Free Playing

Activity:

Spend some time today simply playing an instrument. Do it without any intention or goal. Just explore. String together melodies and chord progressions. Sing gibberish. Try to simply enjoy the sounds you make.

If you happen to come across something that inspires you, feel free to follow it or let it go.

Takeaway:

I have friends that have a guitar or a piano but aren't exactly musicians. They enjoy sitting down after work and strumming a few chords or playing little melodies and then they are done. The only point is to enjoy the act of creating sound. It's not meant to serve any other purpose but to relax and unwind.

I often spend so much time trying to create something that I forget the joy of creating. Sometimes it's nice to just make a little sound! Taking the time to enjoy playing music on the simplest level can be very inspiring, refreshing, and relaxing. Spend a little time every once in a while simply enjoying the therapeutic benefits of playing music.

Day 192: Try One of Your Techniques

Activity:

During this course, you have been accumulating a Reference File called "Techniques to Try in a Song." Today, pick one and try it out! Spend some time using any of these techniques as the basis of your songwriting today.

Takeaway:

There isn't much point to collecting information and ideas if we never use them. Do your best to experiment with one of your techniques today. Don't feel like you have to cross it off your list when you are done. It's likely that the Techniques to Try in a Song can be used in many songs!

Day 193: The Sound of a Painting

Activity:

Choose a painting you find interesting and create music for it. If you can't think of a painting, use "Portrait of Paul Eluard" by Salvador Dali.

The point of this exercise is to use the painting to make musical decisions. What kind of mood does the painting create in you? How might that be reflected in the music? If the painting had a sound component, what would it sound like?

Takeaway:

Imagine the painting you have chosen as a multi-sensory piece of art. You have been commissioned to create the sound. Consider embodying any of the elements of the painting and tell its story with music. This can be a great way to find inspiration for lyrics too!

Day 194: Mind Map

Activity:

A Mind Map is a graphical way to organize ideas. The central idea is placed in a circle in the middle of a page. Subtopics are each in circles around the central idea. Details about each subtopic are in circles around the subtopic.

Here is an example from Mindtools.com: https://www.mindtools.com/media/Diagrams/MindMaps_Figure3.png

Create your own Mind Map, using one of your Song Titles from your Reference Files. Place the title in the center and in the subtopic circles place related ideas. Around each subtopic put details about those related ideas.

Takeaway:

I find a Mind Map to be helpful when I am first coming up with a song idea. I generally try to get as much information as I can on the page. A lot of times the subtopics become ideas for verses.

The process is also very useful when you are creating metaphors. Suppose I am trying to compare life challenges to mountains. I write "mountains" in the center and related elements about mountains in the subtopics, such as "valleys." The details circles will contain information about the subtopic like "low point," "rock bottom," "shadows," etc.

Having a visual for my ideas helps me while writing the lyrics.

Day 195: Pick Presets by Name

Activity:

Compose some music today with presets you choose based on their names only. Go through your instruments and effects, choosing only presets with names that catch your attention; don't listen to them first. Once you choose it, you must use it! It can help to come up with a theme before you start choosing.

Takeaway:

By giving yourself a strict constraint like choosing sounds based on their names and then being forced to use them, you must then come up with creative ways to make them work. There's no backing out! You must move forward! This technique has a subconscious effect of making you feel a little less responsible for the results of what you make because you are stuck with the sounds. Sometimes this can be just the edge you need to take the pressure off and get things done!

Day 196: A Character's Perspective

Activity:

Pick a character from a movie you love.

Try to imagine that you are in the head of that character as he/she is freewriting in their journal. What would they write about? Try to focus on the character's feelings, wishes, hopes, desires, and conflicts. Don't be too specific about the other characters and elements of the film. It might help to replace those names and elements with pronouns like he, she, it, they, etc. Really try to put yourself in that character's shoes and explore their emotional state.

Takeaway:

The point of this activity is to gather ideas for songs and song lyrics. If you write any lines you like or come up with concepts for songs, collect them in the appropriate Reference Files (Song Titles and Song Scenarios are likely candidates). By trying to see the world as other people and characters might, we can come up with fresh new ideas for our songs.

Day 197: The Number One Song

Activity:

Look up what the number one song in your area is. Listen to it and make a list of things you notice about it while listening. See if there are any ideas you can borrow. Add any ideas to your Reference Files (Song Scenarios, Chord Progressions, Song Titles, Techniques to try in a song).

Takeaway:

Even if it's not your normal style of music, see if you can learn something from this song. There are lessons in all kinds of music, and many great genres were created by combining two seemingly unrelated styles.

Day 198: Something from the Number One Song

Activity:

Pick any aspect you noticed yesterday while listening to the current number one song. Try to create a piece of music using that aspect, but make sure nothing else about the music is the same. Use a different key, tempo, rhythmic pattern, genre, etc.

Takeaway:

I find when I make a track that is attempting to use one particular musical idea, I often make progress faster. It's because there's at least one thing about the song that I am certain about. Figuring out something you can build a song on top of is very helpful!

Day 199: Object Writing

Object writing is when we freewrite around a specific object. Focus on the five senses. Delve into memories and associations. Personify the object. Give it desires and aspirations. Don't judge what you are writing. Feel free to wander away from the original object. If the pen stops moving, return to the original object and choose one of the five senses to focus on.

Activity:

Spend five minutes doing some object writing. Your object today is: a pencil.

Once you have finished, look for any material that can be used for song ideas. Add these to your Song Titles and Song Scenarios Reference Files. Feel free to explore any interesting lines as song ideas or lyrics. Be on the lookout for lines that you might take out of the context of the original object. Applying the characteristics of one thing to a completely unrelated thing can be the basis for interesting metaphors in your writing.

Takeaway:

It's ok if your object writing takes on a symbolic meaning. It's ok if you wind up somewhere completely different. It's ok no matter what happens, as long as you keep going!

Day 200: The Sequel to a Song You Love

Activity:

Pick a song that you love. Preferably one that fits your current state of mind.

In your notebook, write down a few of the standout elements of that song. These might include the drum beat, the vocal melody, the overall mood, the transitions, the contrast between parts, etc. You can also take note of the chord progression (you can usually find these by Googling the song title and "chord progression") and sounds. Feel free to add any ideas to the appropriate Reference Files.

Considering some of these elements as a starting place, try writing a sequel to this song. What happens next in the story? Where do the characters in the song go next? What happens to the music next? Try to keep the connections somewhat loose. You are just trying to make a next chapter or a sibling or a distant relative to the original song.

Takeaway:

I always think having a song in mind or even a concept or some kind of goal is a great way to start writing. It can spark ideas and automatically removes a lot of other possibilities and directions. It's a way of limiting your options. It's ok and probably best if your song wanders from the original. Many songwriters use other artists and their music as inspiration for their own work. See where your inspirations take you.

Day 201: A Roll of the Dice

Activity:

Go to Google's "Roll Dice" page: https://g.co/kgs/M1Hfzc

Choose the 8-sided Die. (You can use a real die if you have one)

Roll 2 times.

Use these numbers to create a chord progression in a key of your choice. For example, if I rolled 3 and 8, in the key of C major, this would translate to E minor and C major.

Takeaway:

In this Roll of the Dice challenge, you only get 2 chords! If you feel you need more, try altering the chord a bit the second time they come around. Maybe your chords are E minor and C major, then they become E minor 6 and C major 7. This can turn your 2 chord progression into a 4 chord progression.

Day 202: Add an Ostinato

Ostinato is a musical phrase that repeats. Usually the chords or bassline will change underneath, but the melody stays the same. Sometimes the bassline plays an ostinato while the chords and melodies change.

Let's add to yesterday's Roll of the Dice exercise.

Activity:

Now that you have created two chords with yesterday's activity, try creating an ostinato melody. Play the melody once over the first chord, then repeat it exactly over the second chord.

Takeaway:

Ostinatos are interesting musical devices because although they stay the same, their character changes with the chord changes. This can spice up your chord progressions quite a lot!

Day 203: 3 Ways to Create Contrast

Activity:

When we are trying to create new sections of our songs, it's important to create contrast. Find a piece of music you've been working on that needs a new section. Take a look at the notes in one of the instruments, perhaps the bassline. Try these three things:
- Change the note lengths. If your part is mostly short notes, give the next section longer notes.
- Change the note rhythms. If your notes are fairly straight, give them a more staccato movement.
- Change the distance between the intervals. A part that makes big melodic leaps can be contrasted with a new part that makes smaller movements between notes.

Takeaway:

The best way to let the listener know there is a new section of our song is through contrast. By creating contrasting sections, we give the listener something new to pay attention to. Then we can return to our previous part and the listener will feel familiar with it.

Day 204: The Ways Harmonies Interact

Here are a few ways two instruments can play melodies together (Put these in your Techniques to Try in a Song Reference File):

Parallel Motion - Melodies move together and maintain the same interval. (If the notes are a 5th apart, they maintain that relationship as they change notes).

Oblique Motion - One note moves while the other stays on the same note. (The bass walks down the scale while the singer stays on the same note).

Contrary Motion - The notes move in opposite directions. (The bass goes down and the vocal goes up).

Similar Motion - The notes move up and down together but the intervals change. (The bass goes up a 3rd but the vocal goes up a 5th).

Activity:

Choose any of the above types of motions and write music for two instruments (perhaps a bass and a lead). Strictly adhere to the type of motion. Try to come up with a 16-bar phrase.

Takeaway:

Having some rules to follow can help focus our writing. Experiment with the different types of motions and see which ones sound best for your idea.

Day 205: Create a New Motion

Activity:

Revisit the 16-bar phrase you came up with yesterday using one of the types of harmonic motions. Now come up with a new section using a different type of motion. This time, try for an 8-bar phrase.

Takeaway:

A great way to create contrast in our writing is to change the way the instruments interact with each other. By changing their relationship to each other the new section will feel new.

Day 206: Oblique Strategy Day

Activity:

Having specific restrictions and limitations is one of my favorite ways to work. But sometimes something more abstract will take us in unexpected directions.

Brian Eno's "Obliques Strategies" are perfect for this type of inspiration. They are all up to your own interpretation. It's likely that your interpretation will depend upon the project and how you are feeling in the moment.

Visit the Oblique Strategies online here: http://stoney.sb.org/eno/oblique.html

Use your prompt to create some music today. Interpret it as you like. You can apply it to a project you are working on or start something new.

Takeaway:

The "Oblique Strategies" can spark ideas you wouldn't ordinarily have, just like when you collaborate with others. In a way, these cards allow you to collaborate with an abstract idea. Go with whatever comes to mind!

Day 207: Random Word Generator

Activity:

Let's continue with finding inspiration from abstract ideas.

Go to the Random Word Generator: https://randomwordgenerator.com

Use the word you get as inspiration for your music making today. What associations come to mind? Any ideas for songs? Try not to think too hard and jump right in!

Takeaway:

Sometimes a brief brainstorming session is helpful here. Write down your thoughts and idea and see if any of them make for useful song ideas. The key here is to work fast. Quality is not a concern!

Day 208: Odd Bar Lengths

Activity:

Most popular music is in phrases that last 2, 4, 8, or 16 bars. It might be a chord progression that goes for 4 bars or a riff that is 2 bars long. Generally, sections change after 8, 16, or 32 bars.

Today, challenge yourself to make music with an unusual bar length. Try 6, 10, or 12. If you are feeling adventurous, go for an odd number like 5, 7, or 11.

Takeaway:

Sometimes we can break our habits and patterns by going against the conventions. By creating music of unusual bar lengths, we can tap into chord progressions and melodies we wouldn't normally try. Our lyric writing will have different patterns and stresses.

Day 209: Whole Tone Scale

Activity:

The Whole Tone Scale is made up of only whole tone intervals. If we begin at C, we build the scale by moving up two notes until we are back at C. The C Whole Tone Scale is C, D, E, F#, G#, A#, and C. It's an unsettling scale because none of the notes feel like home. For example, if you started the Whole Tone Scale on any other note in the C Whole Tone Scale, you would get the same notes. For example, E Whole Tone is E, F#, G#, A#, C, and D, which are the same notes as the C, D, F#, G#, and A# Whole Tone Scales.

Here's a short video about it from Berklee Online: https://youtu.be/MotdhW3mMVM

And here's a piece I created for a day in the Jamuary challenge to make a new jam each day during January. I really leaned into the unsettling feeling of the scale: https://soundcloud.com/brianfunk/13-no-more-whole-tone

Today, compose some music using the Whole Tone Scale. While it's unlikely that this scale would fit into your normal style, try to pay attention to the moods and emotions this scale can evoke. It helped me to imagine I was creating music for a film that called for a feeling of instability and disorder. I imagined someone who was recently dumped by a lover imagining all of the things they will never do together again.

Tip: Because the Whole Tone Scale is so unfamiliar to me, I found it very helpful to set my MIDI controller to only play notes within the key. I also used a pitch correction plug-in on my voice set to the Whole Tone Scale.

Takeaway:

Forcing myself to make music with the Whole Tone Scale taught me that if we want to create unusual and strange emotions, we might want to try unusual and strange scales. Part of the fun of this experiment was I didn't expect to get much out of it. This relieved a lot of pressure and led me to learn new techniques and applications for unusual approaches.

Day 210: First, Last, Best, Worst (Friend)

Activity:

First, Last, Best, Worst is an idea generating activity I learned from Mathew Dicks' phenomenal book on story telling, *Storyworthy*.

Today we will focus on friends.

In your notebook, write down the name of your first friend, last (most recent) friend, best friend, and worst friend. Then take a moment to recall any memories about each on the list. You might be surprised at the things you remember, and they might lead to good ideas for songs.

Takeaway:

The First, Last, Best, Worst activity can be done with anything (boy/girlfriend, pets, cars, guitars, homes, etc.) It will inevitably churn up memories and within those memories might be great song topics.

Day 211: The What Not To Do List

It's easy to get caught up in patterns and habits when we make music. Let's try to come up with some things not to do so we can keep our music fresh.

Activity:

Think back or listen back to some of your recent music. Are there certain things you rely on? Do you use particular sounds or instruments often? Are you favoring certain musical keys and scales? Perhaps you stay within a particular tempo or time signature. Maybe you use certain chord progressions a lot or you always make 2 or 4 chord progressions. Do you use the same effect or plug-in too often?

While there is nothing wrong with using similar approaches (sometimes those become our signature), trying to do things differently will open up new possibilities.

Make a list of at least 3 things that you do often and call it "What Not To Do." The next time you are feeling stagnant in your music, try these rules out!

Takeaway:

By actively trying not to do things we rely on, we are training ourselves to find new techniques. Ultimately, it is ok to do the same thing more than once. Many artists have made their careers doing their thing the way they do it repeatedly. But try to challenge yourself to move outside your comfort zone. You might find something new that you can then rely on in the future!

Day 212: Use Your What Not To Do List

Activity:

Make some music by following the rules of your What Not To Do list from yesterday.

Before you start, it might be helpful to come up with some alternative approaches. If you always write in 4/4, try 6/8. If you always use white noise risers, thing of something else you create to build energy and tension.

Whatever you chose, stick to your rules. You have already discovered that those old techniques are effective. Now try to find new ideas that you can add to your arsenal.

Takeaway:

When we first begin making music, everything we try is new. If we are lucky, we find a few things that work. It can become easy to rely on those workflows, but if we stop experimenting, we might stop growing.

Day 213: Make The Entire Beat First

Activity:

Build the beat for the entirety of a song before moving on to anything else. Create the differences between sections, transitions, and dynamics. Think of it almost like an instrumental of only rhythmic elements. It might help to listen to a song you like and pay close attention to the drums/percussion. Get all of the details right before moving on. Treat it as if you are not permitted to go back and change anything later.

Takeaway:

Often, when I am writing music, I start with a short drum loop or maybe a chord progression. Then I start adding other elements on top. I don't really know much about the duration of the song, the dynamics between sections, or where it will go next. I'm simply sketching things out.

Other times, I've sat down at the drums and recorded a beat to an imaginary song. I change the beat where it feels natural and play simple fills to stitch the parts together. Then I write the other instrument parts on top of the drums.

The benefit of this approach is that I have already determined a length, as well as the different sections of my song before I even touch another instrument.

This was one of my rules for my *Country Punkin* EP. https://soundcloud.com/brianfunk/sets/country-punkin

My other rules were:
- Record all sounds with one microphone attached to my Teenage Engineering OP-1.
- Boil the song down to the bare minimum (no instrumentals, intros, or outros).
- Start by recording a drum beat.
- Write the song on guitar or bass on top of the drum beat.
- Restrict myself to the 4 tracks on the OP-1.

It was a surprisingly quick and fun process. Since my beat was set, everything else had to fit it.

This approach of starting with a beat will help you make decisions and commitments, which will give your work a forward momentum.

Day 214: Inspired By a Sound

Activity:

An important element of many styles of music is the sound of the instruments. "Smell Like Teen Spirit" wouldn't be the same if it were performed on a banjo. Just about any EDM track falls apart if you replace the bass with a tuba.

Search for a sound that inspires you. You might experiment with guitar pedal sounds, search your sample library, or browse some presets on a synthesizer. Once something pleases you, stop looking and start making music with it. Try to let the sound itself guide your musical decisions.

Takeaway:

My favorite part about getting a new instrument is exploring the range of sounds it can make. When I'm disciplined, if I find a sound that inspires me, I start creating. However, most of the time I think, "this will be a cool sound to use one day," then I move on to the next sound. I rarely return to those sounds. When I do return to them, they don't strike me the same way. When inspiration knocks, we have to answer immediately!

Day 215: Create Around the Ambience

Activity:

Wherever you are, go outside or to a window and record the ambient sounds around you. A minute or two is fine (you could always loop it if you need it to be longer). Now create some music on top of that ambient recording. Perhaps you recorded rush hour traffic or birds singing or maybe some people talking. Play some chords, beats, and/or melodies over those recordings. Pay attention to how what you play changes the emotional context of the ambient recording. Think of today as creating a soundtrack for those ambient sounds.

Takeaway:

Sometimes I find the music I record on the computer to be sterile and lifeless. That's because I am placing sounds on a completely silent canvas. Music is never heard in pure isolation like this. There's always some ambient noise and the sound always interacts with the room it is played in. A lot of the allure of vintage tape machines is the sound of the tape hiss. It makes the music sound like it is happening somewhere rather than in an empty digital vacuum.

See if playing over ambient sounds can help to inspire you and bring your music to life.

Day 216: Feeding the Dogs

Activity:

I've recorded a bunch of samples while feeding my dogs in the morning. There are vitamin bottles shaking, scooping sounds, paws running around, and more.

Download the samples here: https://drive.google.com/drive/folders/18_1cWy1p54MlMN55BeE2MHTkTIW3VucJ?usp=sharing

Use these samples to make some music today. Try creating a beat with some of the percussive sounds. Try dropping them into a sampler. Transpose the pitch. Time stretch them. Reverse them. Whatever you can think of is fine!

They can be a focal part in your music or become subtle ear candy.

Takeaway:

I feed my dogs twice a day and it makes all kinds of interesting noise. This is the first time I've taken the time to sample the process. It turns out that there are a lot of useful sounds in there. It should serve as a reminder that sometimes we don't need new gear for new sounds, we just need to pay attention to our surroundings!

Day 217: The Epistolary Piece

Activity:

An Epistolary Piece is a literary work in the form of a letter. It allows the writer to directly address a person and gives the piece a feeling of intimacy. After all, it was written specifically for that particular person. But they often resonate with many different people, because as we have said before, often the key to the universal is the specific.

I find this type of writing also brings out a natural conversational tone. Most people don't speak to others with flowery language and in complex metaphors. So Epistolary writing can be a great way to bring a more honest, sincere tone to our writing.

"Hey Jude" by the Beatles was Paul McCartney's message to John Lennon's son, Julian. But you can also personify nonhuman things as well. Michael Jordan and Kobe Bryant both wrote Epistolary pieces to the game of basketball when they retired. Both letters begin with "Dear Basketball."

By personifying basketball, the letters elevate the game beyond merely a sport.

Try composing your own Epistolary Piece today. You could think of it as a tribute or words of wisdom, or even vent your frustrations towards someone or something. Stay in your own natural voice, as if you were having a conversation.

Takeaway:

The letter you write could very well become the basis of a song. You might reproduce the letter in its entirety or simply pull certain lines. It's a great way to speak from the heart and pull us out of the pressures of writing songs and lyrics.

Day 218: Make Music with Your Birthday

Activity:

Open the Numeric Note Coder (Located at the end of this book).

The Numeric Note Coder is used to turn numbers into musical notes.

Write out your date of birth in the numeric format. For example, May 13, 1997 becomes 051397. In the key of C the notes would be XG CE CDDB.

Use these notes to write some music. You might make them the root notes of chords or the notes of a melody. The choice is yours!

Takeaway:

Sometimes it's nice to just be told what notes to play. There are still a ton of decisions to make, but at least you now have some notes to work with. You might consider tying in some other birthday-related themes into your writing (celebrations, growth, aging, time passing, etc.)

Day 219: A Underused Resource

Activity:

Choose an instrument, plug-in, software, or some other music making tool that you already have but don't use much. Use that as the centerpiece of today's music making.

Takeaway:

We all have tons of tools. Even if all you own is a laptop with Garageband, there are probably many elements in that software you rarely or never use. Experimenting with an underused tool can help inspire us in new ways. It can lead to new workflows. It can also save us money by not buying more stuff!

Day 220: Write About a Human Virtue

Activity:

There are said to be seven human virtues: chastity, temperance, charity, diligence, kindness, patience and humility.

Pick one today and freewrite about it for four minutes. Set a timer. What does it mean to you? Where have you observed it? Where have you seen a lack of it? How does it factor into your life and behavior? Can you think of any circumstances where the presence or absence of this virtue affected a situation?

Read over what you have written and take note of any interesting lines and phrases, as well as topics and ideas for songs. Put anything you get into the appropriate Reference Files (Song Titles and Lyric Ideas, Song Scenarios, Philosophies to Keep in Mind, etc.)

Takeaway:

There are certain universal themes and ideas that just about every song and story tap into. Explore these topics in terms of your own experience and it is likely you will come across ideas that will resonate with listeners.

Day 221: Make A Theme Song for a Human Virtue

Activity:

Imagine the human virtue you wrote about yesterday had a theme song. Today, let's create that song.

Consider the tone of what you wrote. Were your words optimistic? Frustrated? Hopeful? Try to use your perspective to guide the mood of the music. You might also consider how that virtue would be represented musically. For example, humility probably isn't going to have a boisterous, in your face piece of music loaded with pretentious solos and wild ornamentations. But if you were writing about a lack of humility, then those choices would make sense.

Takeaway:

Tapping into universal themes and ideas ensures that your music will be relatable to listeners because we all share these experiences. And since we are working off of our own thoughts and writings about the universal human virtues, we bring our own feelings and experiences to the music, which is a great place to start writing.

Day 222: Challenge of 3s

Activity:

Make some music with the challenge of 3s:
- Only 3 tracks.
- Each track can only play 3 different notes per section.
- Create 3 sections.

Takeaway:

This challenge is incredibly restrictive. It forces you to do a lot with very little. Since we only have 3 tracks that can each only play 3 different notes, we have to really consider our choices. But within those limitations are infinite possibilities. Since we are so limited, we can choose sounds that take up a lot of space in the mix. We must carefully consider the role each instrument plays in the music. This is good practice because, in a world where we actually have infinite tracks and possibilities, it's good to remember that each part of our music should serve a purpose.

Day 223: Thinking in Opposites

When switching between sections of a song, I like to think of them as being opposites.

If section A has syncopated rhythms, short melodic lines that stay on just a few notes, and a particular chord progression, I try to make section B have a straighter rhythm, longer melodic lines, and use chords not found in section A.

Finding ways to do what the previous section did not do is a great way to come up with new parts that sound different.

Activity:

Listen to a piece of music you've made and write down some observations. Do the melodies stay within small ranges? Are certain beats accented? Write down whatever you notice.

Now try to create a new section that does the opposite of those things you observed. Write melodies with larger/different intervals, accent different beats. Try to change at least 3 things about the new section.

Takeaway:

Writing new sections of songs can be challenging, especially if you are producing the entire arrangement before moving on to the next section. No matter what you do next, the new section will sound undeveloped and small in comparison at first. So focus on building the new section using opposite techniques from the previous section. Once you build the new section, you will find it offers something new and refreshing compared to the previous section.

Day 224: Learn from a Song You Love

Activity:

Today we will learn about creating new sections from a song we love.

Choose a song you love and in your notebook make observations about the differences between the sections.

Does the rhythm change? Are sounds added or taken away from the arrangement? What happens to the duration and density of notes in the melodies? Do the melodies cover different intervals and note ranges? What transitional things happen to alert the change between sections (drum fills, white noise risers, change in melody or chords)? Are the chords different? What happens to the song's dynamics? Is the new part louder, softer, faster, slower, etc.?

Add any of these ideas to your Reference File "Techniques to Try in a Song."

Takeaway:

When creating new sections for our music, it's helpful to have a set of techniques you can use. Often just a few changes can make a section feel new and different. Have these ideas and techniques handy so you can refer to them whenever it's time to develop new sections to your music.

Day 225: Percussion is King Today

Activity:

It's fun to change the roles of our sounds every once in a while. Today, make some music where the percussion is the main element. Try to think of your percussion as having a melody. You might even do this literally by tuning tom drums to specific pitches so they can play melodic phrases. This practice is especially common in hip hop with 808 bass drums. You can of course add other types of sounds to the music, but try to keep the drums/percussion as the main element.

Takeaway:

A lot of times music I write is born out of a catchy rhythm. I often try to write drum parts that are almost hummable. Many great songs have been built this way. The drums become a major part of the hook. See if you can make your percussion sing today!

Day 226: The Line Cliche

A line cliche is a melody that descends (or ascends) by half steps over a stationary chord. Usually, it is the root note of the chord that moves, but you can also move the fifth as well.

In "Something" by the Beatles, the verse plays an A Major to A Major 7 to A7. The line cliche here is A, G#, G.

In "Cry Baby Cry" by the Beatles, the chorus has a line cliche over an E Minor chord. The line cliche is E, D#, D, C#.

Activity:

Write some music that contains a line cliche. Within your chords create a melody that moves up or down in half steps. This can create interest in a chord that doesn't change for a long time and can add interesting opportunities for melodies and harmonies.

Takeaway:

Line cliches are very common in popular music and can help add interest and spice to unexciting chords and melodies. Try experimenting with unusual chords over your line cliches. I particularly like how the Beach Boys did this in "Kokomo" and how Jake Lizzio explains it: https://youtu.be/etNHA3RhDo8

Day 227: A Way Out of The Loop - Subtractive Arrangement

Activity:

One of the most common questions I hear from students is "how do I move from an 8 bar loop to a full song?" In truth, I have countless 8-bar loops covered in dust and rust on my hard drive. I think this happens because it's very easy to write a short loop on one instrument and then start layering sounds on top until the part is completely full. From there, everything you try to add will sound small and incomplete. So we get stuck.

One method that helps is Subtractive Arrangement. Try this on a short piece of music you've abandoned.

Take your 2, 4, 8, or 16 bar loop and repeat it for a few minutes. Think of the full loop with all the instruments playing as your song's climax. Now go through the entire track and delete portions of the loop. Perhaps the song starts with just the keys. Then 4 bars later the bass comes in. After another

4 the drums and lead come in. Try to make sections of your song combining different parts of your loop.

Takeaway:

As a person that loves to start musical ideas in Ableton Live's Session View, I often get stuck with elaborate loops. By using this method of removing parts from my loop, I can start telling a story with the different sounds.

If this is the method you employ, then your entire song will be variations of this one loop. Sometimes that works just fine. You might start adding additional elements over sections that need something fresh. It can also show you where you might need a new section. At this point you will have a better understanding of how that section will function in the context of the song.

Day 228: Sample Your Loop

Activity:

Another way to make use of our unfinished loops is to treat them like a sample.

Try exporting your loop into a single file. Think of it almost like recording a sample from a vinyl record. In fact, you might consider processing your loop through some interesting effects before exporting it. I like to add a vinyl or tape plug-in to give it the sound of an old recording.

Now bring your exported loop back into your DAW and start building around it. Try adding a new beat with a drum machine. Chop the loop up into a sampler or Drum Rack. Rearrange those slices into something new. Change the pitch. Time stretch it. Reverse it. Try anything you can think of. See if you can turn your old unfinished idea into something new.

Takeaway:

There have been a number of times when I've been able to create something interesting out of something I had previously abandoned. By treating the idea as a sample, I get a new perspective on the idea and can often take it to another level. Often the new idea bears little resemblance to the original!

Day 229: Share the Melody

Activity:

Come up with a couple of chords and write a melody over them. This might be a great time to use your Chord Progressions Reference File!

Now experiment with sharing that melody with 2 different instruments. You might break the melody in half where one instrument plays the first half and the other plays the second half. You might also try giving the lower notes to one instrument and the higher notes to the other.

Takeaway:

Sometimes our melodies can feel static or unexciting. By sharing it with other instruments you might breathe life into the melody. It can also keep the listener entertained by switching their attention from one sound to another. A relatively simple melody can sound much more intricate and exciting.

I have found this technique especially useful in my 3 piece rock band. I play guitar and sing, and we have a drummer and bass player as well. We only have the option of a few sounds at one time. To help keep things interesting, I'll often sing a line and then play something on my guitar to follow. Rather than strumming constantly and singing over it, I trade between singing and playing. This guides the listener into paying attention to the singing and then shifting to the guitar. It also makes it a bit easier for me to play because I don't have to do 2 things at the same time quite as much! It helps keep our simple arrangement of 3 instruments and vocals interesting.

Sharing is caring!

Day 230: A New Time

Activity:

What times of the day do you rarely make music? Today make music at an unusual time. Perhaps it's first thing in the morning, very late at night, or right after lunch. Simply do your musical work at a different time than normal today.

Takeaway:

Our minds and bodies go through different energy levels and moods depending on the time of day. It's almost like we are different people. By working at different times in the day you might find the way you make music changes. In this course, we are deliberately creating routines and discipline for our music-making. Sometimes breaking the routine changes things up and keeps it exciting and fun!

Day 231: Creating Rhythmic Contrast

Activity:

A great way to create contrast between sections of our songs is to change the rhythm. Take a look at some music you have made that you need a new section for and analyze its rhythm. Here are some ways you can create contrast:

- Change a straight rhythm to a syncopated rhythm (or vice versa).
- Try changing to half time or double time.
- Change the accented beats in the rhythm.
- Change the time signature.

Takeaway:

In order for a section of music to feel different, there needs to be some contrast and change in the parts. Rhythmic changes can be very powerful. They change the energy and flow of the song. Sometimes completely interrupting the rhythm is very effective. Pay attention to how the music you love changes the rhythms and add those ideas to your "Techniques to Try in a Song" Reference File.

Day 232: A Day in the Life

Activity:

John Lennon got the idea for "A Day in the Life" by scanning the newspaper. Let's try something similar today.

Turn on the television or radio to a news program. Grab your notebook and spend the next five minutes jotting down any interesting word phrases or situations for song ideas. See if any of the language or headlines can be recontextualized into a song idea.

Record any ideas into your Song Titles or Song Scenarios Reference Files.

Takeaway:

There are ideas and inspiration for songs all around us. We don't necessarily have to experience everything we write about. In fact, writing about things we haven't experienced can help us get into the minds and feelings of others, which allows us to tap into new worlds of ideas for our songs.

Day 233: Use Our Reference Files

Activity:

We've been collecting ideas in our Reference Files for quite some time now; let's put them to use. Start by choosing a Chord Progression. Try to get a sense of the mood of the chords. Then look to your Song Scenarios. Pick one that fits the mood of the chords. Finally, look at your Song Titles and find one that fits the mood and scenario.
Now start putting together some music!

Takeaway:

Don't worry too much about finding a perfect match. Look for Chords, a Scenario, and a Title that are at least somewhat related. You can do the connecting with the rest of the songwriting. Often ideas don't feel like a perfect fit until we start making the rest of the song. We can write in the connective tissue.

Day 234: Learn One Thing

Activity:

It's likely there is a plug-in, piece of gear, or feature in your software or hardware that you either don't know how to use or have never tried. Spend your five minutes today reading through the manual or watching a tutorial on how to use that particular tool or feature. Experiment and test as you learn. Pause the video or read a few sentences, then try those features out as you learn them.

Takeaway:

It's extremely important that we learn new things for our music-making. We find new workflows that produce music we may never have written otherwise. We speed up our workflow by learning faster ways to do things.

But be aware that often we replace actually creating with learning. This is especially common while watching tutorial videos. Our learning becomes a passive activity. From my experience as both a student and a teacher, not much retention happens if there isn't a lot of activity.

Learning one new thing and working at it and experimenting with it goes much further than reading or watching about a dozen new things without any hands-on activity.

Day 235: Letter to Your Future Self

Activity:

Imagine the person you are today and the person you will be in the future are two different people that can communicate with each other. Write a letter to your future self. You can determine how far into the future you want to go, but make it at least a year. Ask yourself questions. Give yourself reminders. How do you expect to change? What do you hope will be different?

After you are done, read your letter and take note of any ideas for songs, lyrics, and titles. Put those into the appropriate Reference Files.

Then put the letter away. Make an event on your calendar in the future to remind yourself to reread the letter when you are your future self that you wrote to.

Takeaway:

This is a fun activity for setting goals and thinking about what is important to you now and how you imagine your future. It's even more fun when you read it as the future version of your self.

Artists have used ideas like this to craft songs. For example, The Beatles have "When I'm 64" and The Beach Boys have "When I Grow Up to Be a Man." Thinking about your future self can be a great way to come up with song ideas.

Day 236: Rewrite the Lyrics

Activity:

Choose a title from your Song Titles Reference File. Now pick a song in a genre that you think will fit the song title and has a vocal part that you enjoy. Look up the lyrics to the song. Using the patterns and rhythms of the song's lyrics, start rewriting the lyrics, line by line, with you own lyrics that relate to the song title you have chosen.

Pay attention to the accents in the lyrics and try to make sure that important words of your lyric match up with those accents. Follow the rhyming patterns of the original song.

Since you may only have a title when you being, start with that. A great place for a title is the chorus. See if you can fit the title into the same structure of the song's chorus. From there you can work backwards. I like to think of the chorus as the message of the song. The verses help set up the situation that leads to the conclusion or realization in the chorus. Once you have that message, it is much easier to build the story around it.

Takeaway:

This is a great method for writing lyrics because many decisions are already made for you. You have the rhythm of each line, you know how long they should be, and the stresses and accents are already there. I also like that it helps us understand how much time we have to tell the story of our song.

If you are afraid this is cheating, I disagree! Thousands of great poems were written within the rules of the sonnet or haiku, which are just two of many poetic structures that have strict rules about number of lines, syllables, rhyme, and more. The structure helps us fit the ideas within the space. It's like how the size of a painter's canvas helps her determine how large the subjects should be or how a half-hour sitcom is forced to resolve by the end of the show.

I've often come up with decent song ideas by singing along to songs I don't now the words to with my own made up words.

But if you are truly opposed to this idea, then just think of it as an academic exercise. Can you write lyrics that fit the form of this song and deliver your message fully?

Day 237: Make Different Music

Activity:

Let's put our lyrics from yesterday to some music. We can use a similar rhythm and song structure as the song we used to rewrite the lyrics, but we definitely want to change the chords and melodies completely.

I find this exercise works best if we get something simple first. Perhaps we start with a beat that our lyrics will fit over.

I like to think about what the original song did so I can do something different. For example, if the original had a 4 chord progression, mine might be 2 or 8. If the chords changed every 2 bars, maybe mine will change every bar. If the melody of the original lyric moved in an upward direction, maybe mine goes down.

Whereas yesterday we were using the original song for guidance, today we are using it to inform us what not to do.

Takeaway:

As you can probably see, it doesn't take too many changes to make our song sound completely different from the original. We can use this way of thinking on many elements aside from the lyrics. We might hear a beat we like or a chord change that strikes us, or maybe it's the way a song is structure that we enjoy. Use it! We are all standing on the shoulders of those who came before us. Much of our originality will come from the unique way we piece together our influences.

Day 238: Get Silly

Activity:

Today you have full permission to write silly nonsense music. Set aside your artistic self-expression and make something fun and lighthearted.

Perhaps you make a song about your dog chasing her tail or how much your nephew loves dinosaur-shaped chicken nuggets, it doesn't matter. Just allow yourself to make something fun and non-consequential.

Takeaway:

It's very easy to take making music a bit too seriously. We start to feel like everything we do must be some kind of masterpiece or it's not worth doing. It gets too important that we delve deep within ourselves to express something powerful and meaningful. There is often no quicker way to writer's block.

By allowing ourselves to let go and make something that isn't important to ourselves and our identity as artists, we can bypass our judgmental side. We get to practice using our skills without the pressure of making what we create have tremendous significance. It's freeing and liberating.

Day 239: Commit!

Activity:

One thing that prevents us from moving forward is the ability to change what we have already done. While producing a track, we can go back to any instrument and change the effects, the tone, the timing, the pitch, etc. This is especially true when working with MIDI.

Today, let's make music with the theme of committing and never looking back. You might even make the song itself about commitment.

However you like to start, whether it is recording keys, drums, guitar, voice, etc., commit. If you put a nice reverb on a piano chord progression, record the effects directly into the performance. If you program drums with MIDI, record the result to audio. Print effects. Convert MIDI to Audio. Finish a part and move on. Do not allow yourself to go back and change anything! Force yourself instead to work with what you have, always maintaining forward momentum.

Takeaway:

One of the luxuries of modern recording technology is that we can go back to parts we've recorded and change things. But it leaves us in danger of getting caught in a cycle.

If I have drums, bass, and guitar recorded, and I want to add a keyboard part, I might decide to go back and change the guitar part a little. Then once the guitar is changed, I have to change the drums to fit a new rhythm. The next thing I know, the bass is not fitting properly, so I fix that. Suddenly my keyboard part now needs adjustment. Now I'm stuck in the cycle.

By instead committing, I am forced to be creative with what I already have. I can't change my drums, bass, or guitar. I keep looking forward, accepting what is already there. If I am unable to get the keyboard part to fit, maybe it doesn't belong. I'm often amazed at how much better my music sounds when I leave things out!

Of course, there are times when this back and forth is justified. But use today as an exercise in looking forward. A lot of times we go back not because we really need to, but because we are unsure of how to proceed or simply uncomfortable and self-conscious about our music while it is still being crafted. Learn to keep the project moving forward at all times.

Here's an inspiring video on the topic from Robot Koch for Ableton's "One Thing" series: https://youtu.be/Lo7NIt4DqRc

Stay the course!

Day 240: Numeric Note Coder

Activity:

Open the Numeric Note Coder (Located at the end of this book).

The Numeric Note Coder is used to turn numbers into musical notes.

Write out today's date and the current time in numeric form. April 23, 2022 becomes 04232022 and the current time is already in numeric form. Convert these numbers into notes using the Numeric Note Coder.

Use these notes to write some music. You might make them the root notes of chords or the notes of a melody. The choice is yours!

Takeaway:

Let the numbers be your collaborator today! Use the notes given to you to create your music. You might consider using the date for an A section and the time for a B section. Make music you could only make in this moment by using this moment in time as inspiration!

Day 241: What's Changed?

Activity:

Take a look at your Song Scenario Reference Files and pick one. Combine that with one of your Song Titles from that Reference File.

Now in your notebook, brainstorm things that have changed as a result of your Song Scenario. For example, if I'm writing for a Scenario after a breakup, I might write things like "her side of the bed is still made," "empty space in the closet," or "her clothes no longer litter the bathroom floor." Go for quantity. Think of these lines as verse material. Often the verses of a song set the stage.

Now look at your Song Title and consider that for chorus material. The chorus is often where the theme is.

In my Song Titles, I had "She's Gone." So now I will use that as the thematic idea for my chorus. Perhaps I write something like this: "She's gone. Left me for another man. Took everything she owned and ran. She's Gone."

The idea is to simply set the stage in the verse with everyday things that have changed as a result of what you will reveal in the chorus. But don't reveal it until the chorus! That will make the payoff of the chorus more satisfying. The point of our verse is to create a scene that leaves the listener wondering "what happened?" Tell them what happened in the chorus.

Takeaway:

Human beings are curious creatures. We want to know what happened. If we can pique the listener's interest in the verse with captivating images, we might keep them around long enough to want to hear our chorus. The key to making this work is to have specific and interesting details in the verse. A line like "All her stuff is gone" is much less effective than going through all of the specifics of the empty closet, the still-made bed, and no clothes on the floor, because it doesn't really illustrate anything. The closet, bed, and bathroom help the listener picture the situation and try to figure out what has happened.

Day 242: Create a Tracklist

Activity:

There's power in visualization. The more we can clearly imagine our goals, the more likely they are to come true.

It's likely you have aspirations of releasing some kind of collection of music, an EP, a full-length album, or maybe even a double concept album.

Today, write up a track list for this collection of music. Imagine what the song titles will be. You might use songs and ideas you are already working on. You can also select them from your Song Titles Reference File. Decide on a number of songs and list them out in an order that makes sense to you.

Takeaway:

Sometimes visualization gets a bad name. If you dream it, it will not come without hard work. But having the vision in mind is a major step in both beginning and finishing the work. Everything you create starts out with some kind of vision. The more clearly you picture it, the easier it is to turn it into a reality. Putting together a track list, even if the songs are imaginary, can help you get a sense of how the album/EP will unfold. You might start to imagine the energy levels of the tracks. You start to think about beginnings and endings. The project starts to take shape.

Have fun with this! Go into it like a kid daydreaming in school about her band's first album.

Of course, everything you visualize is subject to change. As the goal gets clearer, you may find some ideas work better than others. That's ok. The point is to get it moving.

Day 243: Come up with 5 Titles

Activity:

Today we will continue visualizing our musical release.

Take a look at your track list from yesterday and try to come up with 5 possible titles for the entire collection.

Look for themes or ideas you can connect with your titles. Browse album titles, book titles, and movie titles. Pay attention to the ones that capture your attention. What is it you like about those titles? Do they create an emotion? Do they make you curious about the work?

Takeaway:

We are taking our visualization activity one step further today. Giving a collection of songs a title can help tie the individual parts together. It can even help you write new songs because now you have narrowed your writing down to some kind of theme, even if it is quite loose.

Again, remember to approach this with the spirit of a child imagining the possibilities.

Day 244: Imagine the Album Art

Activity:

Now that you have a track list and a potential title for your album/EP/double concept album, what does it look like?

Looking at your track list and title, write down some descriptive words that come to mind. What kind of feeling do you want your collection to have? What colors work within that vibe? How can you evoke those feelings visually?

You might look at other album covers, book covers, or movie posters. Which ones make you want to listen, read, or watch? What elements in the art make you want to immerse yourself in the world of the work?

You can write these ideas down in a notebook, create sketches, or use computer software to flesh it out a little.

It's not that you are necessarily creating the art now, you are more getting a sense of what the entire package will look like.

Takeaway:

The more we visualize the specific details of our work, the more it becomes a reality. Every album starts out as a vague idea. Slowly the artist adds more detail and narrows the focus until it comes into being.

Having a title, track list, and look for your music might be the very thing you need to pull all of your ideas together.

Day 245: The Seven Deadly Sins

Activity:

The Seven Deadly Sins are Pride, Greed, Wrath, Envy, Lust, Gluttony, and Sloth.

Pick one today and free-write about it for four minutes. Set a timer. What does it mean to you? Where have you observed it? How does it factor into your life and behavior? How might the world be different without it?

Read over what you have written and take note of any interesting lines and phrases, as well as topics and ideas for songs. Put anything you get into the appropriate Reference Files (Song Titles and Lyric Ideas, Song Scenarios, Philosophies to Keep in Mind, etc.)

Takeaway:

Just about all problems in our lives can be traced back to one of the Seven Deadly Sins. They have been present in art and literature for centuries.

Thinking about the Seven Deadly Sins can help us develop interesting and universal ideas for our music!

Day 246: Write for the Sin

Activity:

Using yesterday's free-write about one of the Seven Deadly Sins, find a Song Scenario in your Reference File that fits with that particular sin. As the Seven Deadly Sins are pretty universal, there's probably some situation that fits well.

Now browse your Song Titles Reference File for a title that fits in with the Sin and the Song Scenario. You might even find a song title in your free-write from yesterday.

Use these two elements as the basis of your production today. Feel free to begin however you like: lyrics, beat, chords, melodies, etc.

Takeaway:

Writing from the perspective of a universal idea like one of the Seven Deadly Sins is a great way to begin. Adding in a particular Song Scenario, where you imagine what the situation of the song is and what the listener might be doing while listening to this song, is another major step in making important decisions about the music you are writing. It can help establish things like mood, tempo, scales, etc. The key to making music is making decisions. Narrowing our focus like this is a great way to justify the decisions we need to make for our music.

Day 247: Experimenting with Uneven Rhythms

Activity:

Today we will experiment with combining different length loops in our music.

In your DAW, set up 5 tracks.

On the first track, using the 4/4 time signature, create a 4-to-the-floor kick drum beat (the kick plays on the 1st, 2nd, 3rd, and 4th quarter notes). Boom, boom, boom, boom!

On the next 4 tracks, set up one-bar loops in the following time signatures: 3/4, 4/4, 5/4, and 6/4. (This is easy to do in Ableton Live by changing the time signature of Clips. See image below. I've also included an empty Ableton Live Project you can use (requires Ableton Live 11.1): https://drive.google.com/file/d/1PzKTxOqmgEFuIpTyQtkdBp0tz4Xh8bz5/view?usp=sharing)

Now you can add instruments to tracks 2-5 and start creating patterns in them. As the tracks play on, they will all loop at different times, creating interweaving melodies and rhythmic patterns.

Takeaway:

Most of the time we create music that sticks to one particular time signature. In today's activity, we are experimenting with weaving together multiple time signatures. This can lead to interesting movements and evolution over time. In the way we built our tracks above, even though each track contains a one-bar loop because each loop has a different number of beats, the loops never all repeat the same way at the same time until bar 16!

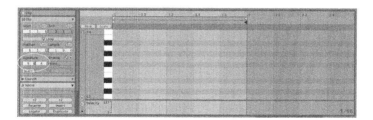

Day 248: Uneven Loops

Activity:

Today's activity is somewhat similar to yesterday's. I find it particularly useful for creating interesting percussion.

Set up 5 tracks in your DAW. You can put any instrument you like on your tracks, but I suggest a simple drum or percussion instrument on each. In my project I used a kick drum, snare drum, rim shot, hand clap, and tambourine.

For the 1st track, create a 1-bar loop. For the 2nd track, create a 2-bar loop. Create a 3-bar loop on the 3rd track. The 4th track will have a 4-bar loop. And finally, you guessed it, the 5th track will have a 5-bar loop.

With this combination of loop lengths, each track will loop at a different time and therefore have a different relationship with the other tracks. The relationship between all 5 tracks doesn't repeat until after 60 bars!

Takeaway:

Creating loops that have different lengths is a great way to create ever changing relationships between our parts. These new relationships can help keep your ideas sounding fresh to the listener.

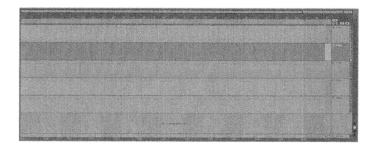

Day 249: Object Writing

Object writing is when we freewrite around a specific object. Focus on the five senses. Delve into memories and associations. Personify the object. Give it desires and aspirations. Don't judge what you are writing. Feel free to wander away from the original object. If the pen stops moving, return to the original object and choose one of the five senses to focus on.

Activity:

Spend five minutes doing some object writing. Your object today is: a handwritten letter.

Once you have finished, look for any material that can be used for song ideas. Add these to your Song Titles and Song Scenarios Reference Files. Feel free to explore any interesting lines as song ideas or lyrics. Be on the lookout for lines that you might take out of the context of the original object. Applying the characteristics of one thing to a completely unrelated thing can be the basis for interesting metaphors in your writing.

Takeaway:

Think of these types of activities as practice shutting down the judgmental side of your mind. The more you can do so, the easier it will be to create without getting frustrated with the end product. The goal is the act itself.

Day 250: Find Rhymes for Your Object Writing

Activity:

Go to an online rhyming dictionary. I like https://www.rhymer.com .

Looking over your Object Writing exercise from yesterday, underline any keywords.

Now enter those words in the Rhyming Dictionary. Write down a few interesting rhymes for each keyword.

Takeaway:

The Rhyming Dictionary is a great tool for finding new words and connections for your ideas. A lot of times we can use rhymes to help flesh out our ideas. Often we wind up in places we never would have found on our own.

Day 251: Create a Rhyme Scheme and Write Around the Rhymes

A Rhyme Scheme is a pattern of rhymes in a work. It is usually written in forms like ABAB, ABBA, ABCB, etc. where each letter represents a sound found at the end of a line.

Activity:

Create a rhyme scheme you will use in your writing.

Now place the rhymes from yesterday's activity at the end of separate lines, using the rhyme scheme.

From here, fill in the words that precede your rhymes. Try to create a narrative around your rhymes.

Move fast and don't overthink it! Think in terms of quantity. You can edit and correct it later.

Takeaway:

Knowing what your rhymes are going to be can make coming up with lyrics much easier. You know where you want to wind up and can then sculpt the rest of the line to fit.

Day 252: Create a Beat for Your Rhymes

Activity:

Create a drum beat that allows you to speak your lyrics from yesterday in a rhythmic manner. Experiment until you found a beat that allows you to speak your lyrics as naturally as possible. Try different extremes in tempo and meter. You might even begin by speaking your lyrics aloud and seeing if you can find a natural rhythm you can build the beat off of.

Try starting your lyrics on the first beat as well as other accented and unaccented beats to see what feels best for your lyrics. Pay attention to what words you naturally accent and how changing the emphasis alters the meaning of your lyric.

Don't worry about melodies at this point. Just try to get a natural rhythm for your lyrics.

Takeaway:

The best lyrics are the ones that flow naturally. By focusing on finding a rhythm to your lyrics, you can ensure that you are emphasizing important words and phrases without worrying about melodies and musical notes.

Day 253: Create Chords with a Pedal Point

Today we will come up with chords for our lyrics using a Pedal Point.

A Pedal Point is a sustained note that doesn't change as the harmony and chords around it change. It's almost like a one-note ostinato. Often Pedal Points happen in the bass, but they can happen anywhere.

Activity:

Choose a note to use as your Pedal Point. Now find chords that share the note in your Pedal Point. Don't be afraid to choose chords that are not all in the same key. Mixing chords from different keys is where this gets interesting.

For example, if I choose E as a Pedal Point, the chords I choose might be E Minor, C Major, A Major, and F#7. All of these chords share the note E, but are not common to any particular key (that I notice right now!).

Takeaway:

Pedal Points can be used to link together chords and melodies that might venture outside of the scale you are in. If you are looking to spice up a chord progression, look for a chord that shares a note with the chord that comes before it.

Day 254: The Number One Song

Activity:

Look up what the number one song in your area is and listen to it.

In your notebook, try to come up with a theory about what the popularity of this song says about our culture right now. Does it reflect some of the issues that are important to us? Is the song representative of any values we share?

This kind of thinking might be great subject matter for your own songs.

Takeaway:

Art tends to reflect the culture it was created in. Art also shapes the culture it was created in. What does our art say about our culture? What would you like your art to say about our culture? What aspects of the number one song can you use in your music?

Day 255: Write in a New Key

Activity:

Choose a musical key that you are unfamiliar with and haven't written in much or at all. It might even be a key that you have dismissed as irrelevant to your music style.

Write a short piece of music using this key.

Pay attention to the feelings the notes create. Is it mysterious? Scary? Tense? Happy? Uneasy? Really lean into those feelings. It might help to imagine that you are writing for a film that calls for those particular emotions.

Move fast and don't overthink it. If you aren't sure where to start, put together 3 or 4 chords from the key and write a melody over them.

Takeaway:

Exploring different keys is a great way to add new dimensions to your writing. Even if you know the key won't fit with your style or genre, you will learn how different combinations of notes create different feelings. Today's exercise isn't so much about making something incredible. Instead, focus on how the different key feels. This understanding will aid you when you want to inject those feelings into your music.

Day 256: Branches and Branches

Activity:

Word Trees can be a great way to come up with ideas and details for a song. In a Word Tree, a central idea is written in the middle of the page. Any related ideas are written around the main phrase, connected by a line. You can then create "branches" from the related ideas you wrote around the central idea. And those sub-related ideas can continue to branch off, and so on.

Create a Word Tree with "Summers of My Youth" written in the center as the central idea. Then surround it with related words. "Beach," "Swimming Pool," and "Bicycle Rides" were a few I came up with, all of which stir up memories and emotions.

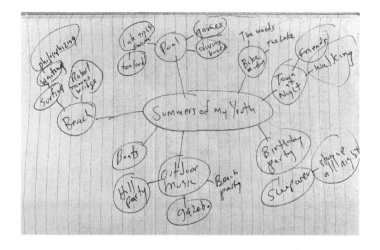

Takeaway:

Sometimes the best way to get a song idea into focus is to brainstorm ideas related to your main theme. Although I started with "Summers of My Youth" as a song topic idea, after a few minutes of creating Word Trees, I feel like there could be an album's worth of material. Digging deeper into a topic helps us get specific with our details.

Grow your ideas!

Day 257: A Roll of the Dice

Activity:

Go to Google's "Roll Dice" page: https://g.co/kgs/M1Hfzc

Choose the 8-sided Die. (You can use a real die if you have one)

Roll 4 times.

Use these numbers to create a chord progression in a key of your choice. For example, if I rolled 3, 5, 2, and 8, in the key of C major, this would translate to E minor, G major, D minor, and C major.

Takeaway:

Imagine you are working with another songwriter and he/she shows up with the chord progression you just rolled. Do your best to contribute to the song idea. Perhaps you can combine this with your Word Tree ideas from yesterday!

May luck be with you!

Day 258: Create an Ostinato with Yesterday's Roll

Ostinato is a musical phrase that repeats. Usually, the chords or bassline will change underneath, but the melody stays the same. Sometimes the bassline plays an ostinato while the chords and melodies change.

Activity:

Use the numbers you rolled yesterday to create a four-chord progression to create an ostinato melody. In the example from yesterday, I rolled a 3, 5, 2, and 8. Those numbers would transfer to an E, a G, a D, and a C. So I would create a melody using those four notes that repeats each time the chords change. I'd play those notes over the chords E Minor, G Major, D Minor, and C Major.

Takeaway:

You'll find that some interesting harmonies can happen as the same four notes repeat over four different chords. For example, over an E Minor chord, which has the notes E, G, and B, I would play a D, which creates a feeling of a 7th chord, and then a C, which is a half step away from B in E Minor. The B will create a lot of tension.

However on the next chord, G Major, that same C note will create a suspended 4th feeling, and the E note will add the 6th.

Each chord will change the feeling of the ostinato melody. If you think there is too much tension or dissonance, feel free to alter the notes of the ostinato over any problematic chords.

Day 259: Creating Contrast

Activity:

When coming up with new sections for our songs, it's important we create changes and contrast.

For today's activity, use the music you've been working on during the last few activities, or pick something else that needs a new section.

Here are 3 elements you can change in the new section to create contrast:

- **Change where the melody starts** - For example: if it begins on a downbeat, begin the new melody on an upbeat or a different downbeat.
- **Change the length of the melodic phrases** - For example: if your melody lasts 4 bars with long notes, try a 2-bar melody with short notes.
- **Change the melodic shape** - For example: if the notes of your melody move up then down, try moving them down then up.

Takeaway:

When creating new sections of a song, pay close attention to what the other sections do, then change a few things. I've heard many producers and songwriters say you need to change at least 3 elements for a section to sound different. While I don't think there's a specific number, 3 is a good rule of thumb. How drastically you change depends on how much you want to change the feeling of your song. If the chorus marks a major revelation in the lyrics, it makes sense to be a little more drastic. But sometimes the chorus leans into the message of the other sections, then fewer changes is probably the best way to go.

Day 260: Stuck? Try an Oblique Strategy

Brian Eno created a set of cards for creative inspiration called "Oblique Strategies." Each card has an abstract statement that is meant to be used to help inspire creativity.

Activity:

Visit the Oblique Strategies online here: http://stoney.sb.org/eno/oblique.html

Each time you load the page you will get a new "card."

Use the "card" you get to come up with some music. It will be up to you to interpret the card's meaning and how to apply it. This might be a bit challenging, but be as creative as possible!

Takeaway:

Today I got "Don't be afraid of things because they are easy to do." I think this is a great reminder to keep things simple. So often when

I'm making music I think about the complexity of my chords, melodies, and rhythms. I forget that I should be focusing on emotional impact and communication. I enjoy creating music much more when I'm not judging what I am doing!

Day 261: One for the Younger You

Activity:

Think back to the kind of music you loved when you were 14 years old. Create something in that style. Feel free to lean heavily on any obvious features of that type of music. Try to make your 14-year-old self proud!

Takeaway:

Often the music that touches us in our early teen years plays a big role in shaping who we are. Although we eventually evolve and expand our tastes, our preferences at that age are often extremely specific. That means that if we were going to make music in those styles, many of the decisions are already made for us! Enjoy trying to fit within the rules and values of your younger self. You will likely learn a lot about the types of things you've grown to love that are not represented in this kind of music.

Day 262: Find Yourself in a Painting

Activity:

Choose a painting to focus on for today's activity. If you can't think of a painting, use Helen Frankenthaler's "Mountains and Sea."

In your notebook, do a few minutes of freewriting about the painting. Pay attention to any feelings that come up. Don't try to interpret the painting, just let it trigger your thoughts.

While looking at the painting mentioned above, I started thinking and writing about a camping trip on a lake I took years ago. Reminiscing about this trip and some of its adventures and misadventures led to a few fun ideas for songs.

Record any ideas for Song Scenarios you come up with. I came up with "Floating on a tube on a lake" and "Arriving at a vacation spot." When you review what you wrote, pay attention for any interesting phrases or words that can be added to your Song Titles and Lyric Ideas Reference File.

Takeaway:

One of the most interesting aspects of art is that its meaning is different for every person that experiences it. We bring our own life and history into the work. Pay attention to how the painting you choose affects you. Rather than trying to uncover something about the art, let the art uncover something about you.

Day 263: Create Music for the Painting

Activity:

Looking at the painting from yesterday, compose some music that captures an emotion it brings out in you. You might refer to your writing related to the painting or simply provide some background music to go with it. Imagine it was hanging in an art gallery and it was your job to create some music to play in the background as people viewed it.

Takeaway:

Creating music to fit another piece of art is a great way to challenge yourself to use your music making skills for a specific purpose. You get to decide what the feeling is and now you must execute. Because we don't really know what the artist of our painting intended the viewer to feel, the music we create combines with the painting and makes new meaning. This type of exercise is excellent practice for film scoring and creating music for commercial purposes.

Day 264: Specificity Leads to the Universal

Activity:

There are said to be seven human virtues: chastity, temperance, charity, diligence, kindness, patience and humility.

Pick one today and freewrite about it for four minutes. See if you can think of a specific circumstance, either from your life or someone you know or even a movie or book. Write about how either the presence or lack of this virtue affected the situation. Get as specific as possible with your details.

Read over what you have written and take note of any interesting lines and phrases, as well as topics and ideas for songs. Put anything you get into the appropriate Reference Files (Song Titles and Lyric Ideas, Song Scenarios, Philosophies to Keep in Mind, etc.)

Takeaway:

Often the best way to get to a universal theme, like a human virtue, is to be extremely specific. The details of the story help bring the themes to life. It doesn't matter whether we have experienced the specific details ourselves, what's important is that we understand the underlying universal themes. That's why we can enjoy stories so far removed and disconnected from our own daily lives. We relate to them because of the universal themes. But we need the specific details to take us there.

Day 265: Put it to Music

Activity:

Focusing on what you wrote about yesterday, create a short piece of music that captures the overall feeling of your writing. Make your decisions based on these feelings. Should the piece have a major or minor feel? Determine the tempo by considering the energy level you want the piece to have.

Takeaway:

It's much easier to begin creating music once a mood and energy have been determined. Using our writing as inspiration can help guide these decisions. It also teaches us what techniques to apply to particular aspects of our music to achieve specific emotional results.

Day 266: The Power Trio

Activity:

Make 3 short loops using only 3 instruments. Try something rhythmic, something to carry the bass, and something for chords and/or melody. Work as fast as possible until you have 3 loops for each instrument.

Takeaway:

The power trio is a common makeup of many rock bands. It's effective because each instrument has a clearly defined role and plenty of room to fill. I often like to start ideas with this type of foundation. Once these elements are created, the rest is ear candy and embellishment on the initial ideas.

Day 267: Write Less

Activity:

Often when we write a song, we want to fit as much as possible into each section. However, it really doesn't need to be that complicated. Generally, one main idea per section is plenty.

Take a look at some of your song ideas from your Reference Files, perhaps a title or a song scenario. Create a simple outline of events for the different sections of the song. You can use the structure of Verse-Chorus-Verse-Chorus-Bridge-Verse-Chorus. Usually, the chorus is the theme of the song, which often contains the title. Now write down one main idea for each of the other sections. Keep it simple and get comfortable advancing the story of the song slowly.

Takeaway:

Sometimes it's nice to give yourself an overview of what will happen in the various sections of your song. This can help you from giving too much information in an early section and then no longer having anything meaningful to say in the remainder of the song.

If your verse details how we fell in love, then you betrayed me, so I left you, there really isn't much left to say. Instead, if verse 1 is we fell in love, verse 2 is you betrayed me, and verse 3 is I left you, we can go into detail in each section. The end result is the listener goes on a journey. Verse 2 is a surprise and verse 3 is a vindication.

Overwriting the early sections of the song prevents us from finishing songs. We don't know where to go because we have already given it all away. Saying less in each section allows you to go into more detail about each plot point.

Day 268: Epistrophe

Epistrophe is the repetition of the last word(s) of a phrase. By repeating the last word(s) of a sentence, we drive your point home.

Here's an example from *The Lord of the Rings: The Return of the King*:

"A day may come when the courage of men fails, **but it is not this day.**

When we forsake our friends and break all bonds of fellowship, **but it is not this day.**

An hour of woes and shattered shields, when the age of men comes crashing down! **But it is not this day!**

This day we fight!"

An epistrophe can cause our listeners/readers to finish your sentence. Often when people are telling us something we already know, we can finish their sentences for them. By manufacturing this feeling through epistrophe, we can create that same sense of agreement, and our writing becomes more memorable in the process.

Activity:

Choose a title from your Song Titles Reference File to use an Epistrophe. Come up with lines that lead you to your title. Every line will ultimately end with the title. See if you can come up with 8 lines in 5 minutes.

Takeaway:

Epistrophe is an excellent way to make a lyric memorable. The listener will quickly latch on to the pattern we are setting up.

Remember, great music is a combination of familiarity and surprise. Epistrophe will help set up the familiarity, but it can also be used to create surprise.

We can change the repeated line at some point, perhaps by inverting it or making it an opposite. Notice in The Lord of Rings example, we are told what the day isn't until the very end when we are told what it is, "This day we fight!"

We can also change the tone of the first half of the lines. Perhaps we were using "... and now I'm on my own" as the ending of each line. We might have started with a negative outlook on being alone. But by the end of the song, we could be glad that "now I'm on my own."

Day 269: Focus on Noun-Verb

In screenwriting, everything is written as simply as possible. The direction is boiled down to the simplest of terms, noun and verb. "Bob runs." "Nighttime." The rest is filled in with dialogue. This is because many of the other decisions will be made later by producers and directors. The Noun-Verb technique leaves out any extra words and gets right to the point.

Activity:

Try the Noun-Verb technique to outline lyrics ideas for the sections of your song. Usually, there isn't much need for more than one main idea per section. Once you have the simple Noun-Verb outline of your sections you can begin to flesh them out lyrically.

Takeaway:

We often get overwhelmed with the details of making music. It's easy to get an idea and then quickly feel the burden of coming up with rhymes, rhythms, production choices, arrangements, etc. Imagine coming up with an idea for a movie and then suddenly worrying about film location, casting, scoring, lighting, promotion, and whatever else goes into making movies. It's too much at once. That's why screenwriters focus on the bare bones of Noun-Verb.

By instead focusing on the big picture, we can make the large decisions that help the smaller details fall into place. If one particular detail has us stuck, we can choose to work on a different aspect. Often once a few other things are in place, we find the solution to that part we were stuck on.

Day 270: Go on an Adventure

Activity:

Your job today is simple and there is no requirement you produce anything special. Spend your five minutes making music someplace else than your normal environment. Go outside. Sit on a park bench. Visit a coffee shop. Stop by a friend's house. Just change the scenery. Bring your instrument, laptop, or just a notebook and be creative somewhere new. Make the goal to work someplace different. The product or output doesn't matter. If you get something nice, great. But as long as you work somewhere new you have succeeded for the day.

Takeaway:

As important as routine is, breaking it can lead to new ways of thinking. You might decide to sample some background noise or a street light that makes an interesting sound (True story: https://brianfunk.com/blog/2019/10/2/street-light-synths-free-ableton-live-pack-186). You might recognize human nature in squirrels hoarding nuts for the winter. The conversation you overhear might have statements you can use as song lyrics. Or you might come back with a renewed appreciation for your normal workspace. All positives!

Day 271: Plan a Schedule for a Project

Activity:

It's Day 271. We've been collecting ideas, experimenting, and developing strategies to make music for 270 days. That leaves us with 95 days. 95 days is plenty of time to finish a project. So let's make a goal to finish a collection of music within the next 95 days. 95 days from now, you will have something to show for your efforts.

Today, let's realistically plan how much time we can give to this project. That will help us to determine the scope of the project.

To give some perspective, for my band's recent project, we got together once per week for 3 hours. As a rule, everything had to be created while we were together, so we worked completely from scratch. In 3 months we were recording 4 songs.

If you can give 3 hours per week (once a week or an hour 3 times a week), that would come out to be 42 hours in our remaining 95 days. That's just over the equivalent of one full 40-hour work week. That would be plenty of time to finish a collection of a few songs.

So for today, plan a schedule for the next 3 months. Put it on your calendar and stick to it.

My band made Thursday evenings at 5:30 our designated time. We negotiated this time with each other and our families. It went on our calendars. I removed Thursdays from my availability to speak with podcast guests. I don't make plans for Thursday evenings. We are simply unavailable at that time. If for some unavoidable reason a Thursday doesn't work for one of us, we figure out an alternate time as soon as possible. Our go-to alternative time is Saturday at 2 PM. Locate an alternate time for yourself; things will come up.

Takeaway:

I cannot stress the importance of scheduling your music-making time. The people I know that do this get things done. The people that don't never have enough time. You have been doing these activities for 270 days; making music is obviously important to you. Dignify it with a regular piece of your schedule.

If you are worried about the time commitment, consider this: by putting it on your calendar, you are designating a time to focus on your music. That also means you are designating time when you *don't* have to worry about your music. This will save you from the constant pressure of making music and the guilt of not doing it. Having a time when you turn it on allows you the rest of the time to turn it off.

A key differentiating factor between people who finish music and those who do not is the schedule. Those who get things done turn it on regularly and consistently at a specific time. Those who do not always think they will find time later or feel like there is never enough time. Decide to be the former and make a commitment you can adhere to.

You can do this.

Day 272: Plan the Project

Activity:

Now that you have figured out how much time you will give to your musical project, let's figure out what that project is going to be.

As an example, let's stick with the 3 hours per week, 42 hours in the next 14 weeks. You may have designated a different amount of time. I think 3 hours per week is completely reasonable. It adds up to quite a bit of time without being overwhelming. But the choice is yours.

If we go with the example of my band, it took us 3 months of 3 hours per week to write, rehearse, and record 4 songs. Somewhere in the middle of our 3 hours, we usually took a 15 minute break. I consider the break important and necessary so we won't subtract it from our 3 hour block. I recommend you schedule a short break if you are working more than 90 minutes at a time.

That means that each song took us roughly 10 hours.

In that time we wrote everything from scratch. We pursued and ultimately discarded or postponed other possible song ideas while getting to the 4 we liked best.

You have a solid 270 days of these activities to draw from. That may help you work a little faster.

My bandmates and I have written and recorded songs together and separately for many years. You may have more experience or this might be your first proper project.

Consider these factors and determine what a semi-realistic project might look like. Do the math. If you want to do a 10 song album, that's about 4.5 hours per song. Does that sound reasonable to you?

Write down your plan in your notebook. Make it real. Figure out where you will need to be at the halfway point, about 46 days from today. If you are doing a four-song EP, that means either 2 songs finished or 50% of the way through each of the 4. Get as specific as possible with your plan.

Takeaway:

You may have noticed I said "semi-realistic project." I think it's ok to try for something slightly ambitious because if you fall short, you still have something significant. But don't make it too large. Realizing you are nowhere near where you need to be could be devastating enough to make you quit.

On the same token, if you are planning something that will take much less time than you have, you will likely procrastinate and justify skipping sessions.

The point is to get a plan down that is achievable and challenging. Once we decide on something and start setting it into motion, it begins to take shape. We start to clearly see what needs to be done and we can do it. Get your plan together and then we can get to work!

Day 273: Make a Playlist of Ideas

Activity:

Spend some time reviewing some of the ideas you've collected during our activities over the past 272 days. It's likely that this is quite a big undertaking, so we will do it over a couple of days. Go through some of your projects, song ideas, recordings, and sessions. Bounce down any idea that excites you into an audio file that you can listen to on your music player. Create a new playlist called "Project Ideas."

Takeaway:

It's important that we sift through some of our ideas for our project. You probably have some pretty good ideas in various stages of completion. Start collecting them in one place. This will give you an idea of what you are working with and it will also help you find ideas that will work well together on an EP or an album.

Day 274: Continue Making Your Playlist

Activity:

Pick up where you left off yesterday. Go through your ideas from our activities and bounce them into files you can listen to on your music player. Add them to your "Project Ideas" playlist.

If you have any other potentially good ideas from the past, you can add them to the playlist as well.

Takeaway:

After today, we should have a pretty good idea of what our ideas are. They will all be in one place and the next step will be narrowing down which ones we want to finish.

Day 275: Start Examining Your Playlist

Activity:

Now that we have our ideas in once place, we can start examining them. Put on your playlist in the car, while going for a jog, or straightening up your living space. Ideally, listen to them while doing something else so you aren't hypercritical of your work. Remember these are probably baby ideas. They still need nurturing and development.

As you listen, notice which ideas strike you. Which ones get you excited to finish them? Which ones have the most potential?

Also, pay attention to which ideas go together well. Do any share similar styles, genres, and/or themes?

Rank your ideas based on these types of criteria. I like to use three categories: Definitely, Maybe, and No.

Takeaway:

Listening to our work in a casual way can help us take in the main ideas, feelings, and energies of each piece. We can experience our music more as a listener than as the creator. That can help us from getting lost in the details and being too critical of our ideas in their early stages.

Day 276: Determine Which Ideas Make the Cut

Activity:

Be prepared, this can be a difficult part of the process.

Today we will decide which ideas we will pursue for our project and which ideas we will leave behind.

On Day 272, you planned your project. You determined how many songs you could reasonably work on in the amount of time you have designated. It might be a 4-song EP, a 10-song album, or a 7-part rock opera.

Choose the ideas from your "Project Ideas" playlist that you will use for the project.

It's time to commit! These are the ideas you will work on finishing in the remaining 89 days!

Write them down in your notebook. Make them real. It's hard to overstate the power of putting this to paper. You might even make a couple of copies and post them in a few places where you will regularly see them. This will help motivate you and keep you focused.

Takeaway:

Making the decision on which ideas you will pursue is a difficult one. It often means leaving behind perfectly good ideas simply because other ideas will better fit the project. Remember, you can always come back to these ideas for another project in the future. But for now, we need to focus on the ones we want to finish.

Don't skip the step of writing down the songs for your project. In order to create a collection of music, you have to make it out of thin air. Every little thing you do brings it out of your head and into reality. This first step of writing down the ideas is crucial. It helps you visualize it into being.

Look at your project written down on paper proudly. You are going to will this into existence through consistent effort and determination. Every step of the way, even ones that feel like setbacks, will bring you closer to this reality.

Respect the importance of achieving this step. It is the foundation upon which the entire project will be built!

Onward we go!

Day 277: Musical Note Coder

Open the Musical Note Coder (Located at the end of this book).

Each letter of the alphabet has a corresponding musical note.

Activity:

It's likely one or many of your ideas need development. Select one you wish to work on and think of a word that encapsulates the theme of the idea. Use each letter of the word in the Musical Note Code to come up with some notes for a new section or element within your song idea.

If you get notes that are not in the key of your idea, you can round them up to the nearest note in your key (ex: an A flat/G sharp would round up to an A in the key of C major). Or challenge yourself to incorporate those notes into your idea. You might be surprised how a note outside the key can color the emotion of the music.

Takeaway:

Again, a little chance can help us move forward. Allowing some randomness in can open new doors of opportunity. Try to keep an open mind about what chance brings you. Imagine as if it is a collaborator that is very excited about an idea and it is your job to make it work.

Day 278: Random Word Generator

Activity:

Go to the Random Word Generator: https://randomwordgenerator.com

If you need an idea for a song, see if you can use this word to get one. Otherwise, try to apply this word to an idea you are working on. Spend some time freewriting in your notebook. What kind of connections can you make to your idea?

I got the word "year" and it helped me consider aspects of time in my own writing. I began thinking both how much can change and how much can stay the same in a year's time.

Perhaps the word you get can help you come up with a new section of your song. In my case, "Year" worked well as the theme for a bridge where I changed the timeframe of the lyric to the future.

Takeaway:

A little bit of randomness can help guide our ideas into new directions. They can also be the piece that finishes the puzzle. Even if you think your word might not work in your song, explore it anyway. Sometimes the tangents we wind up on as a result of our word can be exactly what we need. And if nothing else, it might yield material that works well for a future idea.

Day 279: Break it into Smaller Pieces

Activity:

Take a look at each idea from your project playlist. In your notebook, make a list of what each idea needs in order to be completed. Try to break down each step you want to take with each song. Here are a few ideas: Write lyrics, record drums, create a bridge, work on the arrangement, create transitions, mix, etc.

Takeaway:

It can be daunting to try to complete a collection of music. Now that we have the big picture, it's important that we get down to the smaller pieces of the project. This will give us specific items to work on. We can chip away at the project piece by piece until it is finished.

Keep in mind that you may discover additional items that need to be completed or you might decide that you don't actually need to do certain items on your list. These discoveries are progress.

Even setbacks are progress. And there will be setbacks. Just remember that once you are faced with one, you will be forced to figure out a way around it or through it. That is part of the process. Just keep moving!

Day 280: Apply a Deadly Sin

Activity:

The Seven Deadly Sins are Pride, Greed, Wrath, Envy, Lust, Gluttony, and Sloth.

Choose one that applies to any of the song ideas from your project playlist. Free write about it for a few minutes in your notebook. Think about how it can connect to any song ideas you have. Use these ideas to come up with lyrics and make musical choices. Keep in mind that you can also write positively about any of the sins, for example how you or someone else has overcome them.

Takeaway:

This activity is a freewrite with a purpose. You are specifically trying to develop a song idea by applying a broad theme to it. The more we can narrow in on an idea the better its chances of getting finished. Keep drilling down on the idea until it gets clear. Then only keep ideas that serve to reinforce the theme of the song. Everything else should be removed.

Day 281: Give Your Song a Job

Activity:

In order to find the themes and messages of our songs, it helps to figure out what the song's job is. Why should it exist? What is it going to do for you and the listener?

In your notebook, consider the following questions about this song:

- What is the song's conflict?
- Does it offer a solution to the problem?
- What type of mood are you trying to create?
- Does the song provide a soundtrack to the mood or does it change a mood?
- What activity would a listener be doing while listening to this song?
- What is the song not?

See if you can pigeonhole the song as much as possible. Try to clearly define its purpose. Allow it to be a particular kind of song. Allow it to not be other kinds of songs.

Takeaway:

By clearly defining what a song is about, what it is not about, and what its purpose is and its purpose is not, we can visualize it clearly. That's an important step to finishing. We are literally pulling songs out of thin air. Once we have it, diving deep into its purpose will help us make it a reality.

Day 282: Why Does it Matter?

Activity:

Spend some time today freewriting in your notebook about why making music is important to you. Consider the project we are working on for the last section of these activities. Why does it matter if you finish it? How will it benefit your life? Will it affect others? How will you feel when you have it finished? How will you feel 27 years from now knowing you finished this project (and hopefully many more to follow)? How will this help you on the next project? In what ways does making music improve your life and well-being? How would your life be different if you weren't or never made music?

Takeaway:

It is inevitable that we go through periods when we lack inspiration or feel a sense of pointlessness to our work. When there are so many problems in life and the world, how can we justify sitting around making our little sounds? These thoughts often stagnate projects and deplete our determination to move forward.

It's extremely important that we have our reasons and motivations clearly defined for these moments. Remembering that music has lifted us out of difficult situations, motivated us to work out a little harder, helped us stop to appreciate the beauty in life, increased our connection with other people, and helped us not feel so alone can be enough to reignite our spirits. It can help us push through those dark moments of self-doubt.

Doubt, insecurity, and inadequacies will creep into our minds as we create. I promise. It's part of the process. Keep your writing about why making music matters handy for those moments. The darkness will set in on you. Be prepared with your purpose and use it to soldier on.

Here's a podcast I made as I was desperately trying to claw myself out of these struggles: https://brianfunk.com/blog/whymusicisimportant

Stay Strong!

Day 283: Creating Contrast

Activity:

Pick a song you are working on that needs a new section.

When creating new parts to our songs, it's important to create contrast. Below are a few ideas to try.

- Change the density of melodic parts (more notes or fewer)
- Change chord rhythms and lengths
- Use different chords/avoid chords from the previous section

Evaluate the idea you already have and come up with something new using the principles above.

Takeaway:

For a new section of a song to sound new, it needs to change. Of course, too much change can be jarring, but changing just a few elements is often enough to make the change pleasing. Keep these ideas in mind by recording them in your Reference File "Techniques to Try in a Song."

Day 284: First, Last, Best, Worst (Kiss)

Activity:

First, Last, Best, Worst is an idea-generating activity I learned from Mathew Dicks' phenomenal book on storytelling, *Storyworthy*.

Today we will focus on kiss.

In your notebook, write about your first kiss, last (most recent) kiss, best kiss, and worst kiss. Then take a moment to recall any memories about each on the list. You might be surprised at the things you remember, and they might lead to good ideas for songs.

Takeaway:

The First, Last, Best, Worst activity can be done with anything (boy/girlfriend, pets, cars, guitars, homes, etc.) It will inevitably churn up memories and within those memories might be great song topics. It's not important that you cover each item (first, last, best, worst), do the best with the ones you can remember.

Day 285: Collect Your Tools

Activity:

Set aside some tools you will use for your project ideas. Pick a few pieces of gear, instruments, and plug-ins that will be the go-tos for this project. Is there an instrument you've wanted to make use of? Did you download samples or plug-ins that you'd like to get to know better? Use the project as an excuse to learn these devices.

If your DAW has a favoriting system, use it for this purpose. I often allocate a few of my Collections in Ableton Live's Browser to a project I'm working on. Those tools become my palette. Here's how to use Ableton Live's Collections: https://help.ableton.com/hc/en-us/articles/360000268570-Using-Collections-

Takeaway:

Today we have nearly infinite options at our disposal. We can spend hours testing out countless samples, plug-ins, and loops. While this is truly amazing, it can slow us down and prevent us from moving forward. I've lost creative momentum trying out multiple compressors, EQs, and reverbs on a sound. Most of the time these are details that don't make that much of a difference.

By setting aside a go-to compressor, EQ, and reverb, I can choose it and move forward. If there's a reason to use something different, I can make that decision later in the process. Most likely, it won't matter.

Aside from working faster and not getting caught up in the details, having a limited set of tools allows us to get to know those tools better. We start to understand their subtle details and personalities. At the very least, our project will help us learn our tools.

Day 286: Get Some Inspiration

Activity:

Find a breakdown or analysis of a great song. There are plenty of YouTube videos on this topic. If you aren't sure where to look, try the "What Makes This Song Great" series on Rick Beato's YouTube Channel or listen to the Song Exploder podcast. Both will likely cover at least a few songs you like, but it almost doesn't matter; there's always something to learn.

Be on the lookout for interesting workflows, techniques, or musical ideas. Add these to your Techniques to Try in a Song Reference File.

Make it a point to use at least one idea in your project.

Takeaway:

A behind-the-scenes look into a great song will teach us and inspire us. Often, I'm amazed by the simple things that make it into a song. Watching these types of song breakdowns is a great way to inspire yourself and give yourself new ideas to try in your own music.

Day 287: So, But, Therefore

Activity:

The creators of *Southpark*, Matt Stone and Trey Parker, gave a talk on plot development in which they explain how they follow the "So, But, Therefore" formula for writing episodes of the show (you can likely find it by Googling "Southpark so, but, therefore"). The first scene of the show will be the "so this happened" part. The next scene introduces some surprise and conflict "but this happened." The next scene will show the result of those occurrences, "therefore this happened." They try not to connect scenes with "and." "This happened and this happened and this happened" is boring and doesn't show much interaction between the events of the story.

We can use this formula for writing our lyrics.

Think of your verses as "So." Explain the situation.

The chorus can be "but." Something got in the way. The plan changed. A surprise occurred.

The bridge can then be the "therefore." Therefore this happens as a result of the surprise.

Take some time with a song idea and try to structure it in this format. For now, don't worry about the lyrics, just the plot points.

Takeaway:

Giving a song structure like this can help us shape the narrative of the song. It prevents us from giving too much information up front and allows us to give each change in the song a change in the narrative. Using the "So, But, Therefore" method ensures that each new part of our song develops the story. There is progression and direction. It helps keep it interesting and may keep listeners staying until the end of the song.

Day 288: Ouija Boarding

Activity:

Ouija Boarding refers to the game where spirits supposedly give players secret messages by gliding a reader over letters and numbers on a board. For our purposes, Ouija Boarding is a type of freewriting where we are "possessed" by an idea and try to write down anything related to that idea.

Choose one of your song ideas you are working on and write down anything and everything you can think of that relates to this idea. Listen to your idea and feverish write down anything that comes to mind. How does the song make you feel? Do any images come to mind? What are the emotions associated with the sound? If you have lyric ideas, jot down words or phrases that come to mind.

Don't worry about grammar or spelling. The more you write the better. It's a game of quantity.

Once you have finished, underline or circle any words or phrases that you think fit the idea. Use these to identify your song thematically. Try to determine what the song is and what it is not.

Takeaway:

It's likely you will start to see some connection between ideas. Focus on those connections. Leave stuff out that is unrelated to the main theme. The point is to try to make clear decisions on the song's identity. This will help us make musical choices as we develop the idea.

Day 289: The Elevator Pitch

Activity:

An Elevator Pitch is a short description of an idea that any person could easily understand. It comes from the idea of running into a boss or investor in an elevator and telling them your idea before the elevator ride is over and the person leaves.

In plain language, write the elevator pitch for one of your song ideas. You might use the song idea from yesterday's Ouija Boarding activity. Be sure to define what it is and what it is not. Consider some basic and universal themes. Think about what makes the song unique. It might help to imagine you are trying to convince a friend to listen to a song you love. It shouldn't take more than 30 seconds to speak.

Takeaway:

Once I am able to articulate what a song is it's much easier to finish the song. Countless decisions are made based on whether or not they fit the elevator pitch. We are trying to narrow down our idea. This will probably mean it is not for everyone. That is usually a good thing.

Day 290: Chip Away at Your Project

Activity:

On Day 279, you made a list of things that need to be done to each of your song ideas to complete your project. If you skipped this step, take some time to do it! Having a list of small tasks can make the project more manageable.

Look at your list and choose an item. You might even pick the easiest thing on the list. Work on that today.

In order to finish the project, we simply need to continue chipping away at the small steps. One step at a time, day after day, and the project will eventually be completed.

Takeaway:

All big things are just a collection of lots of little things. If we can consistently finish the little things, sooner or later the big thing will be finished.

Day 291: A Reasonable Number of Musicians

Activity:

In a world of unlimited track counts and endless plug-ins and samples, it can be difficult to know when to stop adding to a track. We can flood our tracks and overproduce them with ear candy, instrument flourishes, and experimental sound design. After a while, these additions have diminishing returns. Often they soften the impact of the other instruments.

If there are 47 musicians on a stage, 2 of them can probably take a nap behind the drumset and no one will notice. When there are only a few, audiences can pay close attention to what each musician is doing. The less we have going on in a song, the more listeners can hear each sound's detail.

When producing a song, a good rule of thumb is to have a number of elements that a reasonable number of musicians could play. This way of thinking helps us tame the temptation to keep adding to a track.

Pick a song you are trying to finish. Decide on a reasonable number of musicians that might theoretically be performing the music. Perhaps you choose 5 people. From there you know that there won't be more than 5 elements going on at any one moment. That might mean a lead guitar could come in at some point, then later that guitarist is playing an organ part, but there is no guitar. You can give each imaginary musician different roles throughout the song, just not more than one at a time.

Analyze your track and make decisions about each section of the song based on how many musicians you have available to play the given parts. Remember, you may want a section during which some musicians don't play anything!

Takeaway:

Modern technology has taken away many of the limitations that forced artists to call their projects finished, sometimes earlier than they may have wished. But it also enables us to perpetually move the finish line further and further away. We must create boundaries to work within so we don't get stuck in never-ending and ever-expanding projects.

Day 292: Make a List of Opposites

Activity:

In your notebook, make a list of opposites. Up/Down, Good/Evil, Forward/Backward, Easy/Hard, Leave/Stay, etc.

See if you can use each set of opposites to come up with lyrical lines.

Setting up opposites can create an interesting contrast in your writing.

Write a few lines of lyrics using the opposites you have collected. You might even come up with multiple lines for each pair of opposites. Get as many as you can.

Examples:

I am looking up to you as you look down on me.

It feels so good to be so bad with you.

It's bad in a good way.

Every step forward is two steps backward.

Takeaway:

Statements with contrasting words work a little bit like rhymes. They set up an expectation. Ideas feel complete and are memorable when they contain opposites. These types of statements are especially powerful in lyrics and songs that have some kind of conflict of ideas and feelings.

Day 293: Give Your Opposites a Home

Activity:

Take a look at the lines you wrote yesterday containing opposites. Review your song ideas and see if any of the lines could potentially fit into these songs. Consider the general themes of your ideas and think about ways you could interpret your lines to fit those themes. Use this as a starting point for your lyrics or perhaps to complete unfinished lyrics in your song.

If you can't find a use for the lyrics, at least add them to your Song Titles/Lyrics Reference File

Takeaway:

We want to finish music. In order to do that, we need to make decisions. Do your best to make use of some of the ideas you came up with yesterday. You might have imagined a world in which an idea of yours is realized perfectly, but that is just a fantasy. We need to make it a reality, and that usually means our fantasy will become imperfect.

That's ok. It's better to finish an idea and move on to the next one (and do that repeatedly) than it is to linger with ideas in a state of incompletion.

Day 294: Letter to Your Past Self

Activity:

What advice would you give your younger self? What do you know now that would have helped you in the past?

Take a few minutes to write a letter to your younger self. Choose an age and write as if you could speak to that younger version of yourself. Think about your values at that age. Address any problems you had.

When you have finished scan the letter for any interesting phrases that could be lyrics or song titles, then add them to the Song Titles/Lyric Ideas Reference File.

Takeaway:

A great source of ideas and inspiration for songs is our past experiences. A nice approach to these ideas is with the wisdom we have gained with age. We can use our perspective to create songs that might mean something to others going through similar experiences.

Day 295: Be the Kind of Person You Want to Be

Activity:

In order to be a certain type of person, we have to do the kinds of things those people do. Nobody is simply healthy, intelligent, artistic, or creative. They become those things because of the little things they do on a consistent basis. From my experience, it's almost as simple as deciding to be that kind of person. It's usually not about making Herculean efforts in one sitting, but more about small efforts consistently.

In your notebook, write down the type of person you want to be. Then think about small daily habits that will get you to that point.

For example, here are a few I'm working on that I wrote down. I'm trying to make these things true about myself. Some are new projects and others I have been working on.

I want to be healthy. I'm the kind of person that doesn't miss a workout. I'm the kind of person that makes healthy food choices. I'm the kind of person that doesn't eat processed foods.

I want to be a music producer. I'm the kind of person that works on my music every day. I'm the kind of person that learns something new every day.

I want to be a good person to work with. I'm the kind of person that doesn't get defensive when someone disagrees with me. I'm the kind of person that will listen to other people's ideas and try them out before judging them. I'm the kind of person that doesn't let my ego get in the way of a project's goals.

Takeaway:

I almost didn't write this particular activity because it feels funny writing this down and especially sharing it with others. So I understand if you might think this is a silly activity.

But just give it five minutes.

I can't tell you how many times I've squeezed in a workout, even if it's a 10-minute jog, 50 push-ups, or a few minutes of yoga because I said to myself

"I'm the kind of person that doesn't miss a workout."

What we are really doing in this activity is developing an identity. Our identities are extremely important to us and can often help us act almost automatically. "I'm just the kind of person that does this thing" eliminates the question of whether you should do it or not. It really can help you do something on a consistent basis.

Just be sure to keep it manageable. We can't be the kind of person who works out 4 hours a day, produces music 4 hours a day, calls every person in their family every day, and works 6 jobs. Those kinds of people don't exist! Maybe they exist for one day, but it isn't sustainable.

Consider how helpful it could be the next time you don't feel like making music but you tell yourself "I'm the kind of person that works on their music every day, at least a little bit."

You can do it!

Day 296: No Distractions Today

Activity:

Undoubtedly you've heard of people who have the discipline to remove all distractions while they work. Today, let that person be you.

Turn off the phone, the internet, and the television. Shut out the entire world during this session. If this makes you uncomfortable, do it for just a short period of time. See what you can get done when there is no other option but to work.

Takeaway:

A lot of the activities that have become part of my life and brought me real joy began out of boredom. We never need to get bored these days. We can always occupy our minds with some form of technology that is eagerly awaiting us with clever ways to prey upon our most basic instincts so that we never put it down.

We have to actively make the decision not to let these distractions get in our way.

Try it for today and see what kind of work you can get done. Notice that you probably didn't miss anything important and you can easily jump right back into the river of technology without missing a beat.

Day 297: Think of Your Sounds in Abstract Terms

Activity:

I'm a big believer in the power of imagination in making music. When I first begin playing with synthesizers, my sounds were "clouds floating in the sunset" or "metal robots fighting." I was thinking in abstract terms and as a result, my compositions contained characters and images.

As I've learned more, I've started to hear a filtered square wave at about 2kHz with a tempo-synced LFO modulating the cutoff frequency. Or an 808 snare, with a short decay, detuned by -6 semitones. Not quite as inspiring as clouds and robots!

Choose a piece of music from your ongoing musical project and describe each sound in abstract terms in your notebook.

Maybe your 808 drum beat is an "alien army marching in a parade." Your pitch-shifted and reversed electric guitar is "a meteor shower over a desert sky."

Let your imagination be in control. Try naming your tracks within your session this way!

Takeaway:

When I first started working in a DAW, I didn't have the technical understanding or vocabulary to properly name my tracks. If I were to open my old sessions I'd have names like "Demon Beat," "Insect Chattering," or " Lazer Eyes" (all actual names!). I didn't rely on the technical aspects of a sound to name it because I couldn't. Instead, I let my imagination take control. On some of my older recordings, I still think of the sounds I hear in those terms. It gives my music a little bit of magic.

Reclaim the magic in your music. Use your imagination and let the sounds and textures come to life!

Day 298: Ostinato with Your Name

Ostinato is a musical phrase that repeats. Usually the chords or bassline will change underneath, but the melody stays the same. Sometimes the bassline plays an ostinato while the chords and melodies change.

Open the Musical Note Coder (Located at the end of this book).

Activity:

Use the Musical Note Coder to generate notes using the first four letters of your first name.

Write an ostinato melody with those four notes. That's just a four note melody that will repeat.

Now, paying attention to the notes of your ostinato, write a chord progression that has some of those notes in common. I think it helps to first figure out a key that has the notes of your ostinato. Then create a chord progression with chords from that key.

Takeaway:

Take notice of how your melody feels different over each chord. Listen for any unpleasant dissonances and feel free to change the notes of the chord or ostinato melody to fit. But remember, sometimes it's those dissonances that create a lot of emotion!

Day 299: Object Writing

Object writing is when we freewrite around a specific object. Focus on the five senses. Delve into memories and associations. Personify the object. Give it desires and aspirations. Don't judge what you are writing. Feel free to wander away from the original object. If the pen stops moving, return to the original object and choose one of the five senses to focus on.

Activity:

Spend five minutes doing some object writing. Your object today is: a backyard.

Once you have finished, look for any material that can be used for song ideas. Add these to your Song Titles and Song Scenarios Reference Files. Feel free to explore any interesting lines as song ideas or lyrics. Be on the lookout for lines that you might take out of the context of the original object. Applying the characteristics of one thing to a completely unrelated thing can be the basis for interesting metaphors in your writing.

Takeaway:

Object writing doesn't need to be based in reality or your own experiences. It's just free association. It doesn't need to make sense. Just explore what comes to mind.

Day 300: A Human Virtue at Heart

Activity:

There are said to be seven human virtues: chastity, temperance, charity, diligence, kindness, patience, and humility.

Choose a song you are working on and try to view it through the lens of one of these human virtues. Think of the details of the song as a vehicle to make a larger statement about the virtue you choose. Consider how the song is showing an abundance or lack of the virtue. It might become a bit of advice or a cautionary tale. Use the virtue as a guiding principle for the decisions you make musically and lyrically.

Takeaway:

Nothing helps me finish a song more than having a big-picture theme or message. By analyzing every part of the song through that lens, I can decide whether or not it belongs or if it needs to be changed. Sometimes the thinking is a little abstract. For example, I might write a melody or chord progression that keeps never hits the tonic note of the key, and therefore rarely resolves, in order to depict patience. Let your imagination be free and your interpretations loose. Understanding the big-picture mission of a song can help us make musical decisions and move forward with our work.

PS. It's day 300! Making it this far is a virtuous achievement and certainly displays a few of the seven human virtues listed here. Pat yourself on the back and keep going strong!

Well done!

Day 301: A Roll of the Dice

Activity:

Do today's activity with one of your project song ideas in mind. Try it on a song that needs a new section.

Go to Google's "Roll Dice" page: https://g.co/kgs/M1Hfzc
Choose the 8-sided Die. (You can use a real die if you have one)

Roll 3 times.

Use these numbers to create a chord progression in a key of your choice. For example, if I rolled 3, 5, and 8, in the key of C major, this would translate to E minor, G major, and C major.

Takeaway:

Even if you don't like the chords you rolled, try experimenting with the rhythm and length of the chords. Maybe the first one is 2 bars long and the other chords are 1 bar each. Experiment with different lengths and rhythms.

Day 302: Related Key Words

Activity:

For today's activity, pick one of your song ideas for your project, perhaps the same idea you assigned a human virtue to on Day 300.

Make a list of keywords related to this project. What are the theme and main idea of the song? What are some related topics? Are there any objects in the song? What about people? List anything that is even loosely related to the main idea. Think of it almost like writing tags for a social media post.

Now visit a rhyming dictionary, perhaps this one: https://www.rhymer.com , and find a few interesting rhymes for each word.

Takeaway:

Today we are collecting ideas. It's likely many of them won't be used. That's ok. If we get in the mindset of quantity, we will be less judgmental of each idea.

A great way to expand an idea is to explore related terms and concepts. Often when we make connections to our main idea, we can create interesting lyrics and songwriting choices that reflect those ideas.

Day 303: Build from the Rhymes

Activity:

After yesterday's activity, you have keywords that are related to your song idea, as well as a list of words that rhyme with them.

Write lines of lyrics using your rhymes. Think in terms of quantity again. The more the better. See if you can stay on topic with your main theme. Try to write a line for each rhyme, even if it is cheesy, cliche, or silly.

Takeaway:

Sometimes having the rhymes helps everything else fall into place.

If you already have a rhythm and/or melody for vocals, try to fit your lines in with it.

If you are having trouble finding a rhythm, feel free to think of a song with a lyrical flow you enjoy and rewrite the lyrics using your lines and rhymes.

It's likely that not every line will make its way into the song. That's fine. We can edit later. Now we are simply generating material.

Day 304: A New Place

Activity:

Change it up! Take your music-making somewhere different. Try it outside if the weather permits. Maybe you can work in a different room or perhaps a visit to a friend's house or coffee shop could spice things up. Try to find a different place where you might be inspired in new ways.

Takeaway:

Our environments play a big part in our work. I love having a dedicated workspace, but sometimes a fresh place gets the mind working in different ways. If you feel stagnated in your work, sometimes a new place with a limited amount of gear can be just the thing to spark creativity.

Day 305: The Number One Song

Activity:

Let's see what's happening on the charts!

Look up what the number one song in your area is. Make a list of things you like about it and things you don't like about it. If you like something, add it to your Reference Files (Song Scenarios, Chord Progressions, Song Titles, Techniques to try in a song).

Consider using some of the aspects you like in one of your songs. Alternatively, make sure you avoid doing any of the things you don't like in your song.

Takeaway:

There's a reason a song gets to number one. It has to appeal to a large number of people on some level. Try to figure out the parts you also like and use them in your music!

Day 306: Under-Complicate It

Activity:

The more we learn and the more tools we get, the more we can complicate our music. As pure beginners, we are completely unaware of all of the options and tools available to us. So we just do something and move on.

Spend some time today without using any effects, automation, equalizers, or compressors.

Simply try to create a little bit of music without any of the bells and whistles. Just get the ideas down. Focus on the ideas and don't worry about refining anything.

Takeaway:

In order to make music, we really need to be in the moment and stay on top of our creative energy. When we start sidechain compressing, sculpting EQs, or crafting a sense of space with the perfect combination of reverbs and delays, we slip out of the creating process and start entering the editing process. We start thinking about perfection and getting things just right. It is often the very thing that sucks our creativity away and activates our ever-ready inner critic.

Instead, allow yourself permission to have competing frequencies and a bit of chaos in your ideas. You can always come back to them later and refine it then, after the idea is already present. Becoming critical and looking for ways to edit an idea before it is fully developed is a great way to enter the world of self-doubt!

Keep it simple!

Day 307: Why Are We Listening?

Activity:

Choose a song you are working on for your project, preferably one you are a little stuck with.

Ask yourself, "why would a listener put this song on?"

Try to come up with a specific situation for your song. Maybe it's the song right before you ask someone on a date. Or perhaps it's the perfect soundtrack to a drive home after your favorite team loses the championship.

Write the situation out in your notebook.

You can also add this to your Song Scenarios Reference File. Once you have a good situation, there's no reason you can't write multiple songs for the occasion.

Takeaway:

There's really no music that is good for every situation. However, we often try to write with all of those options open. Determining what our song is for and what it is not for will help us focus our idea. The only way to finish a track is to bring it into focus. Before we make these important decisions, it's just a loose idea with many possibilities. But a song can only be one thing. Decide what it is and then proceed to turn it into that.

Day 308: Turn a Key Word into Musical Notes

Activity:

Now that you have decided what type of situation your song is designed for, choose a word that encapsulates that idea.

To use the examples from yesterday, if it's just before you ask someone on a date, maybe the word is "risk" or "possibility" or "chance."

Or if it's a song for the drive home after your favorite team loses, the word might be "loss" or "defeat" or "resilience."

Plug that word into the Musical Note Coder (Located at the end of this book).

Now you have a few notes that you can try to incorporate into your idea. Maybe these are chord names for a new section or notes for a melody.

If a note does not fit neatly into the song's key, move the wrong note up a semi-tone or two until it fits in your key. But before you change it, see if the note adds a new color to your song.

Takeaway:

Part of the reason we are trying to find a word that encapsulates our idea is to help us focus and clarify that idea. Using the word to generate some notes can help us come up with new ideas and fill in some of the missing pieces of our song. You can think of the connection between the word and the notes it generated as a secret Easter Egg for your song. Perhaps your fans would enjoy hearing this story!

Day 309: Do What a Similar Song Does

Activity:

Choose one of your songs that you are working on for your project that you haven't put into final order yet.

Now find a similar song you like and analyze its structure. Take note of whenever something happens in the song. Make notes of how many bars sections last. Write down when new instruments come in and old ones leave. Take note of whether a vocal melody has long sustained notes or short choppy ones. Take note of as many aspects as you can within a listen or two.

Now see if you can apply those ideas to your song. Be aggressive. Make decisions to either do what the song you are referencing is doing or to not do what it is doing. Then do it. Use the reference song to make yes and no decisions about each section of your song. For example, "The bass doesn't come in until the first chorus. Will I do that with my song? Yes or No?"

Takeaway:

We often get stuck trying to decide how long sections of our songs should be or when to bring instruments in and out. By systematically going through these questions with another song, we can make decisions for our own songs. "Song X did this, I will do this instead."

By using an existing song, we can clarify which questions to ask. It's hard to make decisions when we aren't even sure where to begin. This process can help make the questions clear so we can come up with answers.

Day 310: Make the New Part Different

Activity:

In order for the different sections of our songs to feel different, there must be some contrast. A general rule of thumb is to change at least 3 elements of your song between sections. That is often enough for the music to feel different to listeners.

Choose a song from your project that you feel needs a bit of contrast between sections.
Try using these three techniques:

- Introduce a new sound, instrument, or texture.
- Remove sounds from your mix. The absence of a particular element will create contrast in your new section.
- Change the dynamics. If the preceding section was quiet, slow, or sparse, try making the next section loud, fast, or dense.

Takeaway:

My favorite way to think about creating new sections is by not doing what I did in previous sections. I look for chords I didn't use or simply start the section on a different chord. If I'm coming from a loud part, I might try to make the new part quieter. It's all about doing different things!

Day 311: Your Guiding Principles

Activity:

Try writing out some guiding principles for your work. What are some values or beliefs that you want to have in your music?

For example, when my 3-piece rock band was recording songs for our album, we adopted the principle that it should sound like a live band is playing.

Before we had this idea in place, we weren't sure how far the production would go. Would there be tons of ear candy? White noise risers? Electronic drums embellishing the acoustic drums? Robotic voices and vocoders?

By having the guiding principle of it sounding like a live band, we immediately knew that those elements would not be part of the album's sound. We didn't even have to make the decision. Of course, there would not be vocals drenched in phasers, chopped up, and swirling around the stereo field; it didn't fit with the principle.

Another principle we had was "do more with less." We decided that the least amount of elements was best. So rather than overdub guitar parts for each section or layer guitars to sound bigger, we tried to play each part on a single track or relied on automation to change levels.

Write out a few guidelines that your track will abide by.

Keep them handy as you work. If you are working out a section of a song or trying to decide whether or not to do something, ask yourself whether it fits in with your guidelines.

Takeaway:

Having some guiding principles is a great way to make important decisions. In fact, it actually eliminates the need to even make many of those decisions. Making music involves thousands of decisions both big and small. After a while, it can be exhausting, especially when we have nothing to measure against. Guiding principles give you that measuring tool. Ideas can be accepted and thrown out much easier when we implement them.

Day 312: Try Something New

Activity:

It's likely you have a piece of gear or a plug-in you haven't deeply explored yet. Or maybe there's a feature in your DAW you've never experimented with.

Take a few minutes today to learn about and experiment with something you haven't worked with much before.

If necessary, read some of the manual or watch a tutorial on YouTube.

Then try that technique out in some of your music.

Takeaway:

Sometimes our workflows need a change. Luckily, by just having a computer to make music on, we have more tools than we could ever use. Trying out something new can give our creativity a spark and help us come up with new ideas.

The same is true about learning new production techniques.

But be careful!

It's easy to go into a learning rabbit hole and never apply what we learn. There's a satisfaction to learning new techniques, which can rival the feeling of completing music. It's a much easier achievement, so we can trick ourselves into feeling accomplished by simply learning about new things.

I recommend a 1:1 approach to learning. When you learn something new, apply it to your work. It's really the only way anything sticks anyway.

Day 313: What Would X Do?

Activity:

Think of an artist you love. In your notebook, write down a few characteristics of their style. Do they have certain tendencies musically? Is there something about the way they play their instrument or sing? Is there a type of subject matter they tend to focus on?

See if you can gather a few of their characteristics and try to apply them to a song you are working on. You shouldn't be copying them, just embodying a part of their style.

For instance, I love how Lou Reed has a very conversational lyrical style. His melodies and delivery always sound the way people talk. So in a song I was working on, I focused on delivering the vocals in an almost talking style. It really helped give the song direction and made writing the lyrics a little easier.

Takeaway:

Most of our favorite artists' styles are conglomerations of aspects of their favorite artists. A lot of what makes a unique style is how we assemble our influences into our work. It can be helpful to turn to the aspects of artists we like. The trick is not to simply copy but to take a small portion of their style and give it a try in our work.

Day 314: Use the Worst Sound

Activity:

Search through an instrument you have and find a terrible sound. Now try to use it in your music. See if you can take that sound and make it work in some way.

Takeaway:

I had a cheap Yamaha beginner's keyboard with lots of bad and cheesy sounds. As a guitar player, I always thought the Distorted Guitar sound was especially bad. But one day, as a joke I tried it in a track and it worked perfectly. Something about the sound of this terrible preset sat really well on top of the other real guitars in the song.

Sometimes we don't know if a sound is good until we hear it in context with other sounds. Everything in music is relative. Many sounds are unimpressive on their own, but they may play a nice role in a mix.

Day 315: Take Glory in Someone Else's Win

Activity:

Do you know someone who has accomplished something important recently?

Maybe a friend finished a book or ran a half marathon. Perhaps a family member learned a new skill. Did a former bandmate post a new song on SoundCloud?

Take a minute to reach out to them and congratulate them on their accomplishments. They've done the nearly impossible. They had a mission, they went through challenges and setbacks, and now they have something to show for it. Tell them you are proud and that it inspires you to do your work.

Takeaway:

It's easy to feel jealous when someone else accomplishes a goal. We can easily think of a million reasons why they had it easier and why the world is against us in our goals.

This is poisonous thinking. It is only serving to set us back. It reinforces our excuses and it creates a belief that we can't do it in our present situation.

Instead, do the exact opposite. Find joy in their success. They have proven to you that great things can be accomplished. They have shown you that if you keep at something you will improve at it. They are evidence that discipline and trusting in the process works.

I recently congratulated a friend on finishing his screenplay. I told him "you did the impossible." It's true. So many people have great ideas and beautiful plans they intend to act on once the road of life is freshly paved and full of green lights. Of course, the road of life never is. My friend and I went on to have a great conversation about his work, my work, and what it takes to finish the job. I left feeling inspired and excited. And I could see the pride and sense of accomplishment on his face. Win-Win!

Share in the win!

Day 316: Getting Dressed for the Job

Activity:

A great way to get in the zone for creative work is to make a ritual of it. Routine will help us prepare for the action ahead.

Think of a few things that might help you get in the mood to make music.

Some things I routinely do are: get dressed (pajamas are too comfortable and relaxing), turn on comfortable lighting, do a little bit of stretching and exercise, take some deep breaths when I sit down, meditate, and listen to an inspiring song (often during the exercise part).

Set up a short routine for yourself that will help put your mind in a state to create.

Takeaway:

Surprisingly, small activities like the ones I mentioned above really help me get started.

Getting started is always the most challenging part. But once I take the first step in my routine, which is to get dressed and do some short exercise, I've started the act in motion.

I've heard of people using similar tactics for other tasks, like going to the gym. The goal is to check in at the gym. Then once they are there, they just continue with the ritual.

It's much easier to think about turning on some lights and opening your DAW than to think about the entire task of creating music. Take it one step at a time; usually, after the first few minutes, the enthusiasm will kick in.

Day 317: Another Deadly Sin

The Seven Deadly Sins are Pride, Greed, Wrath, Envy, Lust, Gluttony, and Sloth.

Activity:

Take a look at one of your song ideas for your project. Do any of the Seven Deadly Sins apply to it? See if you can connect the specifics of your song with a universal idea like the Seven Deadly Sins. A lot of times, we can use the big ideas or universal themes as our choruses. What does your song say about the theme? Is there a unique perspective you are shining a light on?

Jot down ideas in your notebook. Try writing a paragraph that states what the song is about. Think about the specifics and the big picture too.

Takeaway:

It's great to write songs about specific situations. They help listeners connect with the music. Making a statement about a universal truth can take it to the next level. It helps make the specifics of a song relatable.

Day 318: We are Halfway Through our Project! How far along are you?

Activity:

Back on Day 271 we started a project that we would try to finish by Day 365 of this course. Right now we are at the halfway point!

Take a look at your plan from Day 271 and Day 272. How far have you gotten? Are you halfway there yet?

It's a good time to consider if there needs to be any changes to the plan. There are still more than 40 days left. Does it seem realistic that you will meet your goal? Do you think you can accomplish more than originally intended? Are you able to dedicate the time you initially planned?

Refine your plan in your notebook. Celebrate the progress you have made, even if it isn't as much as you had hoped. It is more than if you never started! Make some plans for your next actions. If you are stuck, look for some easy wins. Start small and see what you can get done.

Takeaway:

Since we are working on a deadline, it is a good idea to temper our expectations. We can adjust our goals according to our progress and the time remaining. We have approximately a month and a half to go. Hopefully this course has taught you that a little bit every day goes a long way.

Consider how much time you have to spend on the project. See if you can break it down day by day. For example, you might realize that you won't be able to do any work on Mondays and Tuesdays. Factor that into your plan.

Even if you aren't as far as you had hoped to be, there is still plenty of time to get a lot done. Focused work on a consistent basis adds up quickly. Make the most of the time ahead.

I find it especially helpful to consider that the biggest payoff of my efforts might not be the finished project, but the skills and discipline I am building for all future projects. Keep up the good work!

Day 319: Treat Every Minute Equally

Activity:

One of my favorite books on creative productivity is Matthew Dicks' *Someday is Today*. It's loaded with tactics and wisdom that help us find time to complete our creative projects.

The most important takeaway for me was to "treat every minute equally."

We often think that we need chunks of 30 minutes, an hour, or two hours to get any meaningful work done.

Dicks argues that a minute shouldn't be valued based on how many other minutes it is attached to. We should instead collect every loose minute we can find in our day. Dicks writes sentences of his next book during the two minutes it takes for his coffee to brew or the 4 minutes it takes his son to find his shoes before they leave the house.

These loose minutes might seem small on their own but they add up over time. And just as a book is a collection of individual sentences, our music is also the collection of small tasks.

Instead of reaching for your phone while you wait at the doctor's office, open your notebook and work on some lyrics. Plan the tracklist of your next album. Write out a list of priorities for your next recording session.

Spend your day today looking for loose minutes that you can use to inch one step close to your goals. During those minutes you find, plan out what types of activities you could complete when you find them. This way, the next time a 3 minute block comes your way you will know what to do with it.

Takeaway:

I'm willing to bet that you have a wealth of time hiding in loose minutes. 3 minutes of television commercials. Sitting in your car waiting for the person you are picking up. Whatever. Make it a point to use the time productively.

By switching to this mindset, I've become excited whenever I get a moment of downtime. I now have a short list of the types of things I can do when I have a free minute or two.

Another interesting byproduct is that I don't ever really feel impatient. I'm almost happy for the unexpected holdups in my day. They are no longer inconveniences. They opportunities to get some work done.

Make the most of the day!

Day 320: No Ears, Only Eyes

Activity:

Today we will take a drastic measure to help get our songs closer to completion.

Do not listen to anything. We are going to build our song using our eyes only!

Find a song you are working on for your project that is not been arranged over time. Perhaps it is a short loop or a series of loops, or some kind of snippet of an idea.

Place the idea into your DAW's timeline (for example, Arrangement View in Ableton Live). Now drag the idea out over 3 or 4 minutes (or however long you think the song should be). If you have a few idea for different parts, insert those other parts after 16 or 32 bars of the original part. Let that new part go for a certain number of bars (16 or 32 are again good choices).

You can then return to the original idea and feel free to insert other parts you have or repeat sections every so often.

Do this until the entire 3 or 4 minutes (or however long you chose) is filled.

Let your main goal be making the tracks and contents look pretty.

Now go into your sections and strategically remove parts from each section. Maybe you pull the drums out for a bar. Create a number of different combinations of instruments throughout the entirety of the song.

After a few minutes, you can sit back and listen to what you have. As you listen, take notes on anything you like or dislike. Pay attention to what works and what needs adjustment.

Takeaway:

I love this quick and visual way of arranging songs. It helps me plot out my ideas without feeling especially attached to the outcome because I didn't even use my ears. Often I wind up with combinations of sounds and instruments I wouldn't have tried if I was listening. And almost every time I realize that certain parts of my tracks sound better without some of the elements I have created.

Day 321: Transitioning to New Song Sections

Activity:

Find a couple songs you love and pay close attention to where the the sections change.

In your notebook, take some notes on how the music changes.

Are there any instrument fills?
Are new sounds and instruments introduced?
Are elements from the song removed?
Do elements from the new section begin playing a few notes before the change?
Are there noises or effects that help bridge the sections together?
Do the chords or melody change at all before the new section?

The goal is to come up with a number of ideas for creating strong transitions between sections of your song. Add these ideas to your Techniques to Try in a Song Reference File.

Takeaway:

Creating song sections that fit together is often a matter of how they move into each other. A few simple adjustments can make two contrasting parts work together well. Take note of what techniques your favorites songs use and apply them to your music.

Day 322: Smooth Out the Transitions

Activity:

On Day 320 we did some rough arranging without listening. Today let's smooth the edges out a bit.

Pay attention to the parts where things change in your music. We want to spend time creating solid transitions between sections of our songs.

Use your notes from yesterday to come up with ways to connect the sections of your song.

Try creating fills on instruments (especially drums) leading into the new section. Sometimes silence may serve as a fill.

Consider creating some pickup notes to lead into the new section. For example, if a new instrument or sound comes in, try giving it a few notes to play just before the new section.

Allow any instruments that are not in the new section to decay naturally in the new section or give them a final note to play at the start of the new section.

Often a new section only needs something simple, like a cymbal crash or noise swoosh to signify its arrival.

Takeaway:

When connecting the sections of your song, consider whether you want the changes to be smooth or if they should have an abrupt impact. Sometimes the best way to transition is to do nothing at all. Sudden changes can be very effective. Consider the larger themes and ideas of your song, as well as what the lyrics might be saying. Keep your transitions in line with the big ideas of your song.

Day 323: Make a Playlist of Inspiration

Activity:

Take some time to make a playlist of songs that inspire you to make music. Most streaming services allow you to do this. But if that's not an option, create a written playlist in your notebook.

Try to think of some songs that first inspired you to play an instrument or take up songwriting. Add songs that have struck you on an emotional level. Look for music that gets you excited and energized. Find songs that alter your state of mind or help you relax. Put songs that have inspiring sounds on the list.

Get the list going and consider it an ongoing project. After a while, you'll be able to simply shuffle the songs and skip around until something strikes you. Once it does, stop listening and start creating.

Takeaway:

It's important to have inspiration on hand. Having a playlist of songs that make you want to make music can be extremely helpful. When inspiration is low, simply listen to a few songs and let the excitement wash over you. Once it does, stop in the middle and get to work with the feeling of inspiration fresh!

Day 324: Inspiration from Other Art Forms

Activity:

Just as you created a playlist of inspiring music, start a list of other types of art that inspire you. Consider movies, books, plays, paintings, etc. that move you on some level. You might even jot down a few words explaining what you find inspiring about each work.

Takeaway:

Inspiration is precious so we need to be on the lookout for things that inspire us. It may come when we least expect it too.

I read about how Aerosmith were stuck for a chorus in a song they were writing. They took a break to see *Young Frankenstein*. During a scene, Igor tells Dr. Frankenstein to "walk this way." The line got added to the song and the rest is history.

Last night, I watched *Young Frankenstein* and was reminded of that Aerosmith story, which inspired today's activity. Inspiration is contagious! So seek it out and keep track of it for when you need it next.

Day 325: The Sound of a Painting

Activity:

Since we've been discussing finding inspiration for our work, let's turn to a painting one last time.

Today, consider a song for your project that needs more development.

Spend some time looking at Impressionist paintings. (Google "impressionist paintings"). Find something that captures a similar mood as your work.

Think about how you can represent those moods musically. Jot down some notes and apply them to your music.

Takeaway:

We will work with the Impressionists because their work is usually abstract and up to interpretation. Don't feel like you have to "get it right." Instead, trust your intuition and go with what you feel.

Day 326: Sensory Writing

Activity:

Consider a song you are working on and think of a specific time and place that you've either experienced or can imagine experiencing that relates to the song.

Spend 5 minutes describing the situation using the 5 senses. Go into detail about the who, what, when, and where of the situation. Also, consider how you are feeling inside. Things like sweaty palms, heart pumping, or mind racing help show how you feel rather than simply stating it.

The point is not to write lyrics, rather we are collecting specific details about the situation.

As is usually the case with our daily activities, we are concerned more with quantity than quality. Write as much as you can in 5 minutes. Don't edit or question what you are writing.

Takeaway:

By aiming for specificity we can reach universality. While you aren't trying to write lyrics today, many of the descriptions you create will work well for lyric writing.

Once you have finished, review your writing for any interesting lines, images, and descriptions.

Day 327: Give Your Project a Job

Activity:

We've talked about giving your songs a job. It's helpful to consider when a person would listen to a song. All music tends to fit a specific type of situation. That's why you hear all the same songs at weddings, sweet sixteens, and block parties.

The same can often be said for albums and EPs.

Take a look at the songs you are working on for your project (less than 40 days til the end of this course!) and consider what types of situations your songs will work for. Then think about the collection of music as a whole. When would a person put this on? What types of activities might the music fit? What types of moods and emotions will the music complement?

In your notebook, write a few sentences and jot some notes down about when, where, and why a person might listen to your collection of songs.

Takeaway:

In just about every collection of music I've ever made, there came a point when I decided that the music would fit certain situations and moods. Once I have that dialed in, it makes it much easier to move forward. I can decide to do things or not do things based on the goals of the music. Once I have a purpose for my music, it gives meaning to its creation.

That's not to say you can't deviate from the mission a little bit. A great album usually has a range of emotions and energies. But it's within a reasonable degree. James Taylor doesn't have a heavy metal track halfway through his records. Nor do the Ramones have finger-style acoustic ballads on their records.

I don't see this as a limitation on creativity, but rather a focusing of it. Get creative within the range of moods and emotions you've set. If you are writing music that would be great for a workout, consider that every workout needs a little bit of rest. So maybe you have a track that's good for drinking water between sets, or another that is for the warm-up or cool-down part of the workout.

This activity is about focusing your work so you can make decisions and move forward. Music that tries to be everything winds up being nothing. If you have a death metal scorcher maybe save it for another project rather than halfway through your bedtime piano ballads. It's unlikely a listener will want to experience that much disruption. Set up a purpose and world for your music and let the music live within it.

Day 328: Musical Note Coder

Open the <u>Musical Note Coder</u> (Located at the end of this book).

Activity:

Choose a song from your project that you'd like to add additional melodies to or start a new piece of music.

Come up with a single-word theme for the song. It might be something like "growth," "setback," or "possibility," anything that fits in with your song's theme.

Use the musical note coder to come up with a series of notes for your song.

If the notes don't fit within the musical scale you are working in, challenge yourself to make them work (you might find interesting chord changes or create exotic-sounding melodies by using them as passing notes). If that isn't working, you may raise or lower the note to the nearest note within your scale.

Takeaway:

The Musical Note Coder can help get things started, and it may result in ideas we wouldn't normally use. I find it helps me get out of my normal patterns. In reality, it's just a random note generator, but I like to imagine it has special powers. It's as if some kind of destiny is playing a part in my songwriting. When I think this way, it helps tame my inner critic. Since I didn't pick the notes, I'm not as responsible for how they sound. My job instead is to try to make them work as best I can. Sometimes that's enough to get past my own worst critic, my own mind!

May luck be with you!

Day 329: Oblique One Last Time

Brian Eno created a set of cards for creative inspiration called "Oblique Strategies." Each card has an abstract statement that is meant to be used to help inspire creativity.

Activity:

Visit the Oblique Strategies online here: http://stoney.sb.org/eno/oblique.html

Use your interpretation of the card to take a next action on your project. Go with your gut. The first reaction is the right one. Once you get an idea or hunch, go directly towards it.

Takeaway:

The Oblique Strategies are great tools for abstract thinking. The same card can strike you in different ways on different days with different projects. When inspiration is low or you aren't sure where to go. Consider loading one of these cards and letting destiny have a chance as your collaborator.

Day 330: Let It Play a Different Position

Activity:

Sometimes professional athletes have breakthroughs when they are given a chance to play a different position. Babe Ruth started as a pitcher. Today he is known as one of the great homerun hitting champions. Steven Tyler was a drummer before he became the lead singer of Aerosmith.

Choose one of your songs for your ongoing project that needs some extra element. Pick a sound or effect that you wouldn't normally use to do the job.

Need a melodic phrase? Try a fill on the tom drums (this worked pretty well for Phil Collins!). Looking for a soft pad in the background? Try using an aggressive bass patch with a low pass filter on top. Want an effect for the vocals? Try using a guitar amp preset.

Takeaway:

Often the best tool for the job is one that was made for an entirely different purpose. Maybe instead of a typical white noise riser, you record a car speeding down the highway, pitched down an octave. If you are stuck with the normal tools at your disposal, see if something unusual can fit the job!

Day 331: Arrange Like a Sculpture

Activity:

We discussed Arrangement by Subtraction on Day 227. Today is a good day to revisit that method. Let's think of it like a sculptor.

Often, when I am creating music on my computer, I create a drum loop and start layering instruments on top of it. After some time, I might have 8 instruments looping for 4 or 8 bars. This is the perfect time for some arrangement sculpting…

I put those loops in Ableton Live's Arrangement View (this works in any DAW) and drag those loops over the course of however long I think the song might be, generally between 2.5 and 5 minutes.

This long block of loops is my stone. Inside is my song. I have to chip away until I have created some kind of progression in the music.

First I pick a spot where the highest energy point of the song is. I leave this section alone.

Then I start at the beginning of the song and decide which sound will open the track. I delete everything else.

After 8 bars I allow a new sound to come in, maybe more than one. I delete everything else.

The process goes on by carving away sounds every 8 bars until I reach the end of the song.

I'm left with a rough sketch of my song's arrangement.

Choose one of your song ideas that still needs to be arranged into sections. It might even be a 4-bar loop that you never completed. Just make sure there are at least a few different instruments layered on top of each other.

Try the Arrange Like a Sculptor activity with your song.

Do it quickly, preferably within the 5-minute time frame.

Takeaway:

Of course, we are not finished here. It's likely our arrangement is choppy and incomplete. But we at least have something to work with. This is a major step. The song now has form. We have left the curse of the 8-bar loop!

Day 332: Smooth it Out

Activity:

Yesterday we arranged our track like a sculptor. That activity was like using a large chisel. Today we will use smaller chisels and brushes to smooth out our arrangement.

Pay attention to the where the parts change in your arrangement, which was about every 8 bars. Think of ways to smooth out the changes.

Here are a few suggestions:

- Try drum and percussion fills just before the change.

- Let instruments that are taken out play over the change (allow their notes to decay into the next section or let them play one final note as the new section begins).

- Create pickup notes on new instruments that start before the new section.

- Try white noise risers and fallers at the beginning and end of sections.

- Allow reverbs and delays to decay over the section changes.

- Silence instruments for a few beats before the change (works well with drums and percussion).

Takeaway:

Our job today is to make the parts flow into each other nicely. We are trying to blend them together. Often that involves allowing the sounds we are bringing in and taking out to play before or after the change.

Keep in mind that sometimes an abrupt change is nice. Sometimes we want to create musical indications that a part is about to change and other times we want the change to have a sudden impact. Experiment with different ideas and see what works for your song.

Day 333: Build Templates from Songs You've Finished

Activity:

Find a song that you have already finished or nearly finished. Create a copy of that project, leaving the original untouched.

Next remove all recordings, clips, MIDI, and automation from the song. Keep the tracks with any instruments and effects in tact.

You should be left with a project that has tracks all set up with effects, but no sounds.

Save this as a template for future songs.

Repeat the process with any other finished tracks.

Takeaway:

There's no sense doing the work more than once. If you have a finished song, saving it as a template allows you to start new similar tracks quickly and easily.

This approach has been especially helpful for my band. After doing a live recording, I saved the project as a template and use it to record our practices. Every time we play, I open the template and the set up time is almost nothing. When it's time to listen back, everything is already pretty close to mixed.

Having a few goto templates ready can help you get into the creative process faster. You can always alter the template as you go and choose not to use certain elements or add new ones.

Day 334: No Undo!

Activity:

Before beginning this activity, it might be wise to save a copy of your song as it is, just in case you make some serious mistakes!

Open one of your songs for your project. While working on it, don't allow yourself to undo anything. You can only move forward. When you have an idea you want to try, try it and keep going. No looking back!

Takeaway:

The point of today's activity is to move forward fearlessly. In order to finish music, we need to make decisions and commit to them. The undo button sometimes keeps us a little too safe. See what happens when you spend a little time without that luxury. Make sure you have a copy of your project you can go back to in case anything catastrophic happens. With that in mind, do your best to make some major decisions without questioning them. You might find you make lots of progress! Get a little reckless!

Day 335: 30 Days To Go!

There are 30 days left in the 5 Minute Music Producer. Congratulations for making it this far! I hope that you have developed some helpful new habits.

That also means that there are 30 days left to finish the projects we started back on day 271.

Today would be a good day to take stock of where you are in terms of reaching that goal.

What still needs to be done? Does it seem realistic in 30 days? How can you adjust your goal to meet the deadline?

Perhaps if you think you are falling short, consider reducing the number of songs in your project or think of some less than necessary parts of your project you can eliminate. For example, if you wanted to switch out all of the drum sounds, consider keeping them and moving forward.

The thing I don't want you to do is move the deadline!

Imagine that you have to deliver something by day 365. There are people counting on you to do so. Their jobs depend on it. Their families will go hungry if you don't show up with something completed!

If we push the deadline, the project might not ever get finished. But if we change the scope of the project, we can still have something to show for our time and efforts.

If you are on schedule or ahead of schedule, that's great. But it's no time to get complacent. If anything, finish early! Or maybe you can add to the project. Just don't stop working until you get there.

Activity:

Take some time to write in your notebook about the state of your project. Try to list some tasks that need to be completed. Prioritize them. Tackle the most important ones first. It's much better to end up with a project that have vocals that could use a little more compression than it is to not have the track mixed because we spent too much time compressing vocals!

Takeaway:

No matter where you are in your project, there's still plenty of time to make major progress. Even if you haven't even started, 30 days is a lot of time. Keep on working and don't give up on yourself. The point isn't to create the greatest masterpiece ever, the point is to create something. Do the best you can in the time left. Then you can become critical. The time for reflection is after the work is done, not before.

Day 336: Random Word Generator

Activity:

Go to https://randomwordgenerator.com/noun.php and get a random noun to focus on. Spend the next three minutes free writing about this noun. Simply write whatever comes to mind. The goal is to keep the pen moving. If your focus shifts, go with it. Don't fight anything. Just let the words flow.

For the next two minutes, review what you wrote and see if you can apply any of it to the songs in your project. Perhaps there are some lyrical lines or a title in your writing. Maybe some of the ideas can be represented musically.

Takeaway:

When we start writing down our thoughts, we come across new ideas. You might not think you have anything to say, but after spending some time writing, you might be surprised by what comes out. We sort and organize our thoughts by writing and talking. This is why talk therapy is so effective and why therapists recommend journaling. We can use those principles to explore ourselves in our songwriting.

Day 337: Wild Experimentation

I was stuck on a recent project. It was coming along well but I couldn't get the vocals right. I spent a ton of time setting up the vocal chain and recording numerous takes, but they weren't working. I was afraid to do anything too drastic because of all the time I put in.

I made a copy of my session called "(Song Title) Vocal Experiment." I rerecorded the vocals and built the vocal chain from scratch. Suddenly things started to work. I did the same thing for the other songs in the project and the "Vocal Experiment" versions of my sessions became the ones I ultimately finished on every song for the album.

Activity:

Pick a song that has stagnated and save a copy of it. Name the copy "Song Title (Wild Experiment)."

In this copy, try something a little crazy. See how much you can get away with. Do things you'd be afraid to do in the original version. Delete effect chains, experiment with new plug-ins, rerecord parts, etc. Try whatever comes to mind.

Takeaway:

Sometimes we get too used to a project and can't progress because we are afraid we might ruin it. By creating a new copy, we can get a little crazy because we know the original still exists. We always have the original to come back to. See if this approach helps you break through the barriers that may have stagnated the project.

Day 338: Adding Variation

Activity:

In order for songs to stay interesting, they need to have a balance of familiarity and surprise.

It is likely we have parts of our songs that repeat. It probably happens in the verse section or the chorus, or maybe a melodic riff. If we simply copy and paste those sections to create our song, it will likely get boring for the listener.

Try creating at least some small variation each time a section repeats. This might mean that an instrument or sound is added or removed. Maybe there's an extra note or two at the end of a bar. Try a variation on the main melody, for example if the first line ends with an upward melody, try ending the repetition with a downward melody.

Take a look at one of your songs and look for opportunities to create subtle variations in your sections. Keep in mind that a little bit goes a long way. You don't need to completely reinvent the section; you still want it to feel familiar. You just want to give the listener a small reason to listen to it again.

Do this throughout your song in small ways and it could be enough to maintain interest for the entire song.

Takeaway:

It's very easy to copy verse one and paste it into verse two and three. This might be a great way to start, but don't just leave it that way. Make the three verses all slightly different from each other. Whether it's changing a few notes, adding or removing sounds, or changing the energy level, these adjustments will go a long way in keeping your song exciting.

Day 339: Move on Before You're Finished

Activity:

When I am writing and producing at the same time, I often get stuck after coming up with one section. This happens when I've built up the section to near completion. If my first section has all the bells and whistles, anything I try to create for my next section feels weak and unexciting.

The fix? Move on to the next section as early as possible.

Once you have the basis for one section, start the next one. Avoid the temptation to fill out the first part. Working on the next part will help keep your sections at similar stages of completion.

Try this approach with one of your tracks.

Takeaway:

I find it's usually best to progress a song in stages rather than complete one part then move to the next. It's difficult to go from a fully developed idea to a sketch mid-song. Creating new ideas and perfecting ideas involve different modes of thinking. It's usually best to avoid switching mindsets too often in our work. It keeps us coming up with new ideas. Once we have a few ideas together, we can move on to developing those ideas together. The result will often be a more cohesive piece of music.

Day 340: Fill in the For the Rhyme

Activity:

If you have one, get your Rhyming Dictionary or go to https://www.rhymer.com, which is an online one.

Choose a song you are working on and write down five key words that are related to the theme of your song.

Go to the Rhyming Dictionary and find five rhymes for each word. Choose rhymes that you think will best fit your song.

Place each rhyming word on a line at on the right side of a page in your notebook. Create lines that end with the rhyming words. Work fast and don't overthink it. By the end of the exercise, you should have 25 lines that rhyme. (That's a lot for five minutes, so make sure you work quickly!)

Takeaway:

By starting with the rhymes, we get more in the mindset of solving a puzzle. We ask ourselves "what can I fit in these lines?" rather than "What should I write?" This is a much easier challenge!

You don't have to use every line in your song. Choose the ones that fit your idea the best.

Day 341: Think About the Ending

Activity:

Consider how to end a song you are working on. Think about how you want to leave your listener. What are some of the themes of the song? What feelings should the listener be left with?

Here are a few ways to end a song and some of the feelings they might create.

- End on the root or home chord - resolution and finality
- Ending on a strong downbeat - closure, definitive
- Fade out - the subject matter of the song continues on and on
- End on a chord other than the root - unfinished and unresolved
- Abrupt and unexpected stop - surprising and sudden
- Returning to a theme from the intro - we've come full circle

There are undoubtedly other ways (maybe one song transitions into another), so feel free to come up with your own.

What type of ending fits your song best?

Takeaway:

We want to leave a lasting impression on our listeners. It's important to consider how our songs end and what feelings we leave listeners with. A great ending can be the very thing that elevates a song to another level and makes people want to listen again.

Day 342: More Thoughts on Endings

Activity:

Try writing some new material for the ending of your song.

One classic way to do this is to create a tag. A tag is the repetition of a line at the end of the song. "A Hard Day's Night" ends with the repetition of "You know it feels alright."

Perhaps you create an outro that vamps on a line in the song, like "Come Together."

Or end on an unusual chord, like the Major 6th chord at the end of "She Loves You."

You could also stick an unfinished song idea at the end, like the "Can you take me back…" ending of "Honey Pie."

Or maybe a bit of backwards gibberish like the end of "I'm So Tired."

(As you can see, the Beatles were masters at interesting endings).

Takeaway:

It's important to give listeners a reason to listen all the way through. Doing something special at the end of a song can leave the listener feeling satisfied. It makes it worth hearing the whole song rather than just the catchy chorus.

Day 343: Learn a New Technique for Inspiration

Activity:

Take a look at your gear, DAW, or plug-ins, and pick a feature to learn about. Or learn about a new production technique.

Apply that technique or feature to a song you need to finish for your project.

Takeaway:

A great way to make progress on a project is to learn something new and apply that knowledge. It can help move the project along, plus it expands your abilities as a producer.

A great way to stall a project is to keep learning! So be careful not to get caught up in too much learning. Learn something new then apply it!

Day 344: Emotional Impact Above All

Activity:

Today's activity is a shift in thinking.

When putting our songs together, we often try to get everything as perfect as possible. In doing so, we make edits to performances. We remove breaths from vocals, adjust the timing of percussion, or tune every note perfectly.

The mindset of getting everything to sound as good as possible is important at times, but we can't forget that the purpose of our music is usually emotional impact.

When making edits and applying effects, remember that emotional impact is most important.

If a breath on a vocal makes it sound more intimate and personal, keep it in. If a little bit of rushing in the percussion helps build tension, don't quantize it. And if a singer reveals a little hopelessness as the last note of a phrase slides down off the note, let it.

As you are working on your music, remember to let the emotional impact be the most important factor.

Emotion often comes through in imperfections and mistakes. If something technically wrong adds to the energy of the song, consider it right and leave it alone.

Takeaway:

We've all seen videos of virtuoso musicians on the internet. Every note is played perfectly. If that was all that mattered then why don't we only listen to the absolute best musicians?

We have the power to edit and fix every possible mistake in our music. Just be careful not to edit out the feeling. When the emotional energy of a song is right, everything else can be forgiven.

Go with what feels right!

Day 345: Take a Field Trip

Activity:

It's time for a change of scenery. Go someplace interesting and different to make music. Sit on the beach with a guitar. Bring a portable device to the park. Write in your notebook under a tree. Allow the new surrounding to influence whatever you make. Think of an enjoyable place to be and do some creative work there. It might not be the sole purpose of your journey. Maybe you go to the zoo and spend five minutes of your lunch break making a loop on an app on your phone. Create something in a place where your mind is stimulated.

Takeaway:

I didn't go on many field trips in school, but I remember those days better than a majority of the others. The days I've made music in unusual places stick out in my memory among the countless days I work in my normal space. To make something memorable you just need to change one or two elements. Today, see what your creativity is like someplace else.

Day 346: Try Producing for an Audience

Activity:

Staying on task is challenging, especially if we are working on a computer. One way I've been able to stay focused and disciplined is by live streaming my work.

When I know that someone might be watching me, I don't check my email or social media. I won't look for answers on the internet or search for new gear that I think might help me make music. These activities are like running from your problems.

When I am being watched, I simply get to work. I am forced to be creative. I can't hide or search for answers externally.

Try live streaming or screen recording your work today. Don't pay attention to whether anyone is watching or not. Just assume they are. Let the pressure of being watched force you to face the challenges head-on!

Takeaway:

I've turned off my WiFi, put my phone in another room, and even used apps that lock me out of the internet. Although those techniques do help a lot, all I have to do is turn the WiFi back on, go get my phone, and disable the internet blocker. In the challenge of making music, it's easy to rationalize excuses to remove the obstacles that are supposed to keep me from being distracted. When people might be watching and what I am doing is being recorded, I'm much more disciplined. I feel like I have to make progress no matter what.

Give it a shot!

Day 347: Make Music for Someone Else

Activity:

Dedications in books and albums can be great ways to pay tribute to other people. They can also help motivate us to finish our work.

I've spoken to many artists on the Music Production Podcast who've said that dedicating their work to someone they care about helped them find the motivation to keep working on the project.

In my high school English class, one of our writing assignments is a tribute piece. Students must pick someone important in their life and pay homage to that person. It's rare a student doesn't complete this assignment once they pick that person. When they are stuck I simply ask them "you don't have anything nice to say about your grandma?" That's usually enough to get them going.

Pick a song you are working on for your project and pick a person you can dedicate it to. If you really want to raise the stakes and increase your chances of finishing it, tell them you are making a song for them!

Takeaway:

It's easy to make excuses if we are only making music for ourselves. We were tired. Something else came up. We weren't inspired.

But when it's for someone else, those same excuses sound weak and selfish.

I almost always feel more motivated to work on collaborations (even if I am more excited about my own solo projects) because I know other people are counting on me.

We don't like letting people down. Use this to your advantage and make music for someone else.

Day 348: Everything in its Right Place

Activity:

We have less than three weeks before the end of this course, and when your project is due!

Think about what still needs to be done to finish. Gather the tools you will need and organize your workspace with just those tools available.

Chefs operate with the concept "mise en place," which means "to gather and put in place." They gather only the tools and ingredients they need for the job. Everything else is a distraction.

Set Yourself up for success. Get the tools you need to finish your project ready and put everything else away.

Some things to do:

- Put away instruments, gear, wires, etc. that won't be used.

- Create a favorites folder of plug-ins you will need to finish.
- Clean your desk off.
- Make a list of steps you need to take on each song for your project.
- Schedule time to work on your project.

Takeaway:

When I'm recording guitars, it's great to have them set up and mic'ed so I can pick up and go. While recording vocals, it's the same. When I'm ready to mix, all that stuff needs to be put away. I don't want to be distracted thinking about recording or playing guitar. My focus is mixing and my workspace is set up to make it easy to mix and more difficult to do anything else. Putting things away is a big part of this. Remove options. Make the essential tasks easy to begin and all other distractions out of the way.

Day 349: Change the Pedal Point

A Pedal Point is a sustained note that doesn't change as the harmony and chords around it change. It's almost like a one-note ostinato. Often Pedal Points happen in the bass, but they can happen anywhere.

Activity:

Choose a note for a Pedal Point bassline. I suggest the root note of a major key. Now write a few chords over this Pedal Point.

Keep your chord progression the same and try changing the Pedal Point note. Some notes that might work well are the 4th, the 5th, and the 6th.

Notice how changing the Pedal Point changes the mood of your piece. You can use this as two parts of a song.

Takeaway:

Just as changing the chords over a Pedal Point changes the feeling of the music, so does changing the Pedal Point. See what notes fit your song the best!

Day 350: Creating Contrast with Rule of 3's

Activity:

Look at any of your songs that need either a new section or more differentiation between sections.

A general rule of thumb is to change 3 elements between sections. Sometimes more or less is required depending on how drastic each change is.

Below is a list of ways to create contrast. Pick 3 to apply to your song.

- Change note rhythms
- Change note lengths
- Change the distance between notes
- Straight Rhythm or Syncopated
- Half-time/Double-time
- New accents in the beat
- Start melodies on downbeat or on off-beats
- Short melodic phrases or longer ones
- Change melody shapes
- Change the density of melodic parts (more notes or fewer)

- Change chord rhythms and lengths
- Use different chords/avoid chords from the previous section
- New sounds
- New instrument arrangements
- Change dynamics (quiet/loud)
- Change key (relative minor)

Takeaway:

In order for our songs to progress and evolve, we need to create some contrast between sections. Save the list above and add to it as you develop new techniques. Having these on hand while producing makes coming up with new ideas much easier.

Day 351: The Number One Song

Activity:

Look up what the number one song in your area is. By now you've taken notes on a bunch of number-one songs. See if you can find any commonalities and write them in your notebook. Are there any aspects of these songs that are highly unusual? What makes this current number one so popular, in your opinion?

Add anything you like about the song to your Reference Files (Song Scenarios, Chord Progressions, Song Titles, Techniques to try in a song).

Takeaway:

Often a hit song does a lot of things by the book, but has a few tricks that make it stick out too. When making music, we are often balancing tradition and rule-breaking. Pay attention to what the common traits are as well as the unusual aspects.

Day 352: A Roll of the Dice

Activity:

Go to Google's "Roll Dice" page: https://g.co/kgs/M1Hfzc

Choose the 8-sided Die. (You can use a real die if you have one)

Roll 4 times.

Use these numbers to create a chord progression in a key of your choice. For example, if I rolled 3, 5, 2, and 8, in the key of C major, this would translate to E minor, G major, D minor, and C major.

Takeaway:

One last roll of the dice challenge! Do your best to make the chords you came up with work. The dice can be a fun way to gamify your songwriting. Use it when you are short on ideas!

Day 353: It's the Dark Hour of the Soul

Two weeks from now, this course will be over. Your project will be finished and you can enjoy the fruits of your labor.

Today, however, you may very well be in what is called the "Dark Hour of the Soul." You've worked hard and made progress but the end seems impossibly far. You might be unable to imagine possibly finishing your work.

This is normal! It happens to all of us. And the thing that separates those who make it through to finish from those who give up is perseverance and determination. The only way passed it is through it.

Activity:

Make sure you do whatever it is you can to make some progress for each of the remaining days. Focus on the most important aspects. The tiny details can be addressed if there is time. We often focus on tiny details to avoid the big elements.

Don't spend a whole day EQ-ing and compressing drums if your song still needs a bridge!

Take aim at your project's to-do list and check something off today.

Takeaway:

I love asking podcast guests "was there a time when you thought this would never be finished?" There's always an answer and, usually, there are many answers!

Everyone hits this point in their work. Think of it as part of the process. It's like hitting a traffic jam on the way to work. It might slow you down, but you have to keep going.

Keep in mind one of the key philosophies of this course: don't worry about the outcome, worry about the work you put in.

If nothing else, your project will be a major piece in your education and understanding of music making. That is a worthy goal in itself. No amount of reading books, taking classes, or watching tutorials can give you this education.

The actual work you create isn't the point. Moving forward and growing is. See this project as practicing following through. It's the hardest part and it's the only way to make something great.

You can do this!

Day 354: The Layers of The Mix

Activity:

It's important to determine what role the elements of our music play in the composition.

Producers who create the entire song on their own may want every little piece of the mix to play a starring role.

But we need to make decisions about where to place each element.

Choose a song you are working on and in your notebook, categorize each element as being either foreground, middle ground, or background.

In order for one element to stand out, others need to sit back. Decide what the listener should be focused on and place the other elements around the focus.

Takeaway:

If everything tries to be the star, nothing is the star. We need to choose the main element of our mixes and use the other elements to support the focal point.

Keep in mind the focal point may change throughout the song, and possibly within sections.

Having the relationship between your elements set will make the mixing process much easier.

Day 355: Creating Layers in a Mix

Activity:

Now that you've determined the foreground, middle ground, and background, here are some general characteristics of sounds at varying depths. Applying these characteristics to your sounds can help create the separation you are seeking.

Foreground sounds: brighter, drier, higher frequencies, more irregular patterns, lots of dynamic range, usually what the average listener would hum along to.

Middle ground: middle frequencies, brighter than the background, steady rhythmic patterns, more consistent dynamic range.

Background: fewer high frequencies, more low end, more natural reverb, steady patterns.

These are of course generalities but are helpful ideas to keep in mind. You can set elements back in your mix by decreasing the high frequencies, keeping their patterns relatively consistent, and adding some reverb. Likewise, you can push sounds forward by adding higher frequencies, changing up the patterns, and removing reverb.

Consider using these ideas for short times too. For example, an instrumental fill can take the foreground after a line in the vocals.

Takeaway:

Placing elements of the mix in layers will help guide the listener's attention. Remember, you can shift the placement of elements throughout the song too. Try to keep a focal point throughout the piece. It can switch between instruments and vocals, but there should always be something for the listener to pay attention to.

Day 356: Addition by Subtraction

Activity:

We can make space for our sounds by thinking in terms of layers, but sometimes the best thing we can do is remove elements. By taking things out of our mix, we naturally focus our listener's attention and they can pick up on the details and subtleties of a sound.

Additionally, we can remove elements from one section to make the next section more impactful. If we want one section to sound big, the section preceding it must be smaller.

Pick one of your songs and listen to each section with some of the sounds taken out. Try as many different combinations of sounds as you can. See what happens if a sound is removed for the first half of the section only.

Also, consider what the relationship between sections should be. Pay attention to how changing the density of sounds in one section affects the next section. Sometimes what a section needs is fewer elements in the section before it.

Takeaway:

I'm often surprised at how removing sounds from my songs brings things to life. A boring section becomes exciting if I remove the keyboard part in the first half and bring it back in the second half. The climaxes of my songs are more triumphant when the part before it gets sparse and quiet.

Pay attention to how the details of a sound come to life when there are fewer elements surrounding it. Often we find that less is more!

Day 357: A Final Ostinato

Ostinato is a musical phrase that repeats. Usually, the chords or bassline will change underneath, but the melody stays the same. Sometimes the bassline plays an ostinato while the chords and melodies change.

Activity:

Create a chord progression using any chord progression from your Reference File "Chord Progressions."

Write an ostinato melody using the root notes of each chord in your progression. Allow the ostinato melody to repeat over each chord of the progression.

Takeaway:

Ostinatos are really effective musical tools because they create repetition, but the character of that repetition changes every time the chords change. They embody the idea that music must be both familiar and surprising to stay interesting. Pay attention to how common they are in the music you love and see if you can make them work in your own music. Since they are repetitive, they often work very nicely as little hooks.

Day 358: Object Writing

Object writing is free-writing around a specific object. Focus on the five senses. Delve into memories and associations. Personify the object. Give it desires and aspirations. Don't judge what you are writing. Feel free to wander away from the original object. If the pen stops moving, return to the original object and choose one of the five senses to focus on.

Activity:

Spend five minutes doing some object writing. Your object today is: a tombstone.

Once you have finished, look for any material that can be used for song ideas. Add these to your Song Titles and Song Scenarios Reference Files. Feel free to explore any interesting lines as song ideas or lyrics. Be on the lookout for lines that you might take out of the context of the original object. Applying the characteristics of one thing to a completely unrelated thing can be the basis for interesting metaphors in your writing.

Takeaway:

You can complete these exercises with any object. The object isn't really the point. It's more about emptying your mind and seeing what's there without filtration.

Day 359: Plan the Final Week!

There's one week to go in this course, which means it's almost time to finish your project!

Activity:

Spend two minutes looking at your schedule for the week. How much time can you devote to the project each day? This will be the amount of time you have to finish.

Next, spend the last few minutes of this exercise deciding the big actions you can take this week to ensure you will finish on time.

Takeaway:

Thinking we have a whole week to complete something can give us a false sense of what we are capable of doing. Determining how many hours is a much better approach. In seven days, there may only be 5 hours available to work. This is important to know so we can decide to focus on the most important aspects of our work and not get caught up in small details that will prevent us from finishing on time.

Day 360: Unsynced Loops

Activity:

Most music that is created today is synced to a metronome or grid in a DAW. Much of that music contains repeating loops at regular intervals. Sometimes it's helpful to add something that is not so synchronized.

Pick a song of yours that could use a little variation and evolution. Try adding a repeating loop that is not synchronized to the tempo of your track. For example, it could be a melody that lasts 6.3 bars or some kind of atmospheric texture that repeats every 11 seconds.

Unsynced loops will change how the regularly looping material feels because the loops won't repeat in the same relationship with each other.

Takeaway:

Tempo-synced and loop-based music can become a bit predictable. Using unsynced loops is a great way to create variation without much work. It can bring a repetitive section to life and create new musical moments within a song.

Day 361: Experiment with Song Order

Activity:

An important part of any collection of music is the track order. Just as the sections of our songs help build a narrative and journey, the order of our songs creates a longer form journey for the entire project.

Take a look at the songs in your project. Are there tracks with different energy levels? What themes and feelings do you want to use to bring your listener in? How do you want to leave the listener when it is all over?

Write out a potential track order for your project. Then listen to the last 30 seconds of each song and the first 30 seconds of the next. Do you like the way the songs move into each other? Pay attention to the first 30 seconds of the first song and the last 30 seconds of the last song. These are your first and last impressions.

Take notes in your notebook about what works and what does not. Experiment with different track orders until you like what you have.

Takeaway:

The track order determines the story arc of our music. We can use it to take our listeners on a journey. Notice how different a song feels in relation to the music that comes before and after it.

Day 362: Blending Endings into Beginnings

Activity:

Are there any opportunities to blend the ending of one of your songs into the beginning of another?

Sometimes we can let the decay of one song layer over the opening of another song. It might be guitar feedback or delay tails, or you might use some type of field recording at the end of one track that continues into the beginning of the next.

Blending songs together, even just a little bit, helps give a project a sense of continuity and connectivity. It makes it feel less like a collection of random songs and more like a concept. Groups like the Beatles and Pink Floyd used this approach to create concept albums. Hip-hop artists often use interlude tracks and skits to bridge songs together.

Look for ways you might connect two of your songs to help create the feeling of a shared theme and message in your project. Export two songs and place them in your DAW so the ending and beginnings overlap. It works best if there isn't too much musical information like notes and chords. If you want to overlap notes and chords, it helps if the songs are in similar keys. Try using natural recordings (maybe rain or birds chirping) to connect the tracks.

Takeaway:

We can create the sense of a larger theme by connecting our songs together. Even if the ideas aren't explicitly the same, listeners will feel a sense of relationship between the two songs if they are not interrupted by silence.

Day 363: It Only Happens Once

Activity:

Review any of your songs for your project that could use a touch of excitement.

Somewhere in this song, create a musical event that only happens one time. It could be a melodic phrase, a sound effect, a stop, a new sound, or some rhythmic event.

Only allow it to happen one time. Think of it as a special unique moment!

Takeaway:

Sometimes we wind up creating songs that simply repeat the parts that have already played. But it's important to take listeners on a journey. If the listener has already heard everything after the first chorus, what's the point of the next two verses and choruses?

Sprinkle small moments into your music to keep the journey going and give listeners a reason not only to get to the end but come back for those small moments of excitement.

Day 364: Kurt Vonnegut's Short Story Rules

Writer Kurt Vonnegut came up with 8 rules for writing short stories. Although they are often meant to be broken, they can offer a strong framework for effective storytelling.

1. Use the time of a total stranger in such a way that he or she will not feel the time was wasted.
2. Give the reader at least one character he or she can root for.
3. Every character should want something, even if it is only a glass of water.
4. Every sentence must do one of two things—reveal character or advance the action.
5. Start as close to the end as possible.
6. Be a Sadist. No matter how sweet and innocent your leading characters, make awful things happen to them – in order that the reader may see what they are made of.
7. Write to please just one person. If you open a window and make love to the world, so to speak, your story will get pneumonia.
8. Give your readers as much information as possible as soon as possible. To hell with

suspense. Readers should have such complete understanding of what is going on, where and why, that they could finish the story themselves, should cockroaches eat the last few pages.

Our songs are not that different from short stories. We can apply the rules to the actual narrative of our lyrics. And we can apply the rules to the music itself. For example, think of each instrument as a character and the sections like chapters.

Activity:

See if your interpretation of Vonnegut's rules improves your project. Here are some ideas I came up with based on each of the rules. Feel free to steal them and use them in your own way!

Rule 1: Cut down an excessively long intro.

Rule 2: Make the narrator of my lyrics more relatable by showing vulnerability.

Rule 3: Give my melodies a counter melody that fills in where the first melody leaves off.

Rule 4: If a part isn't adding to the emotional impact of the song, it is probably taking away from it.

Rule 5: Present the conflict in the lyrics as soon as possible.

Rule 6: Make sure there is some tension within the music. It builds anticipation for a satisfying release.

Rule 7: Don't try to do everything in one song. Let the song have its own personality and unique features. A song that does too much usually lacks direction.

Rule 8: Try to give as much information in each line of the lyrics as you can. "I saw your face. You smiled; I could tell that you were crying" could just be "Your smile couldn't hide your tears."

Takeaway:

If I had to sum up all of Vonnegut's rules into one, I'd say it's "get to the point." As we reach the end of a project, it's important to go back with a critical eye and edit out anything that doesn't need to be there. More is rarely better. It's better to leave your listener thirsty for more than glad it's finally over.

Day 365: Congratulations!

Congratulations!

Making it this far into this course is a huge accomplishment. You've spent an entire year honing your craft as a music producer. The only way to truly grow and progress is to do the work consistently. No amount of education can bring you this kind of wisdom. You are among the smallest set of people who are able to set their mind to something and follow through on it!

Activity:

Hopefully, your project is finished! Simply finishing is a tremendous accomplishment. At this point, you can look back on your work and take some lessons from it. What worked well? What could use improvement? What approaches were effective? What will you do differently next time?

Write down some important lessons and takeaways in your notebook. Take note of things you'd like to do again and new ideas you want to try next time.

Also, keep all of your Reference Files handy for the future. You've accumulated a ton of ideas and inspiration for all of your future projects. I hope you continue to add to those files so that you can tap into inspiration any time.

Takeaway:

Things that worked well this time might not work so well next time. And things that didn't work this time might be perfect in the future. Keep an open mind!

Having some notes of what worked, what didn't, and what you'd like to try next time is a great way to fuel your inspiration for the next project.

Making music can be incredibly rewarding. That's *because* it isn't easy. There are always challenges and obstacles to overcome. It seems like each time we discover new ways around them, bigger challenges emerge. Try to remember that this is exactly why the act can be so satisfying. So embrace the challenges and be thankful that they are there!

On Day 315, I encouraged you to take glory in the accomplishments of others. Let them be a source of inspiration. Today, take some joy in your own accomplishment!

In that spirit, please feel free to share your work with me. I'd love to hear what you were able to accomplish through this course. It's exciting and motivating to see how you've applied some of the activities in this course to your work. I'd love to hear it!

Celebrate this victory and use that energy to start the next project!

Thank you for taking part in this journey with me!

Congratulations!

-Brian
brian@BrianFunk.com
BrianFunk.com

Numeric Note Coder

Replace the digits of a number with the corresponding musical note to create coded music.

1= Root
2= 2nd Scale Degree
3= 3rd Scale Degree
4= 4th Scale Degree
5= 5th Scale Degree
6= 6th Scale Degree
7= 7th Scale Degree
8= 8th Scale Degree (Octave)
9= 9th Scale Degree
0= Any note you want!

Example: A Major Scale is coded below. 421793 becomes D B A G# B C#

1= A
2= B
3= C#
4= D
5= E
6= F#
7= G#
8= A (Octave)
9= B
0= Any note you want!

Musical Note Coder

Replace the letters of words with the corresponding musical note to create coded music.

A=A
B=B
C=C
D=D
E=E
F=F
G=G
H=A#
I=C#
J=D#
K=F#
L=G#
M=A

N=A#
O=B
P=C
Q=C#
R=D
S=D#
T=E
U=F
V=F#
W=G
X=G#
Y=Any note A-D
Z=Any note D#-G#

Example: "Music" becomes AFD#C#C

About the Author

Brian Funk is a musician and educator from New York. He is a curious sound designer who creates instrument and sound packs for producers that are looking to add unique character and charm to their music. Brian is an Ableton Certified Trainer and teaches music production courses at Berklee Online. He hosts the Music Production Podcast, which explores creativity, technique, gear, and philosophy through informal discussion.

Learn more at BrianFunk.com

© 2023 Brian Funk

Made in the USA
Monee, IL
13 July 2025

21051546R00344